R

GET ON WITH IT

Get On With It

Algy Cluff

Cluff & Sons

First published in Great Britain in 2016 by Cluff & Sons

Jacket artwork and illustrations by John Springs

Edited by Sam Carter

Designed and produced by Tandem Publishing
tandempublishing.yolasite.com
ISBN: 978-1-5262-0150-8
10 9 8 7 6 5 4 3 2

A CIP catalogue record for this book is available from the British Library.

Printed and bound in Great Britain by CPI Group (UK) Ltd, Croydon CR0 4YY.

FOR HAROLD, FREDA, BLONDEL, HARRY,
PHILIP AND CHARLIE

'To be active is the primary
vocation of man.'

Goethe

Contents

FOREWORD

By A. N. Wilson

Algy Cluff has been a good friend of mine for nearly forty years. Only when I read this excellent memoir did I realise how much we had in common in terms of our background. He comes from Cheshire, I from the neighbouring county, Staffordshire; both of us were the children of businessmen, though his father was a much more successful one, commercially, than mine. Napoleon was wrong to say the English were a nation of shopkeepers. They are – or were – a nation of entrepreneurs. The Wealth of Nations – or the Wealth of Our Nation – was built up by enterprising, honest and adventurous people, prepared to take risks. Yes, they made money, but money was not their aim.

Algy, as these pages show, could easily have rested on his father's laurels and followed an early instinct, to read for the Bar, to loll around in gentlemen's clubs and perhaps to dabble in journalism and art collecting. In fact, he had inherited all the energy and courage that was characteristic of Britain in its glory days. After Stowe School he became an officer in the Grenadier Guards, serving with distinction in Borneo and in Africa – a continent with which he has always felt an affinity.

Then there began, after a short spell in the City, Algy's adventurous sorties into the oil industry, eventually broadening out into gold and other minerals. With the fruits of his labours, he bought the shooting estate of Clova, in Aberdeenshire – since exchanged for another estate even further north – and what must be the most charming house in the south of England, his windmill on the White Cliffs of Dover. He has a discerning eye, and early built up a superb collection of modern British paintings – and others. He is also a book collector, and is very widely read, especially in twentieth-century biographies. One of the joys of talking to him is swapping favourite moments in P. G. Wodehouse.

When Algy married Blondel – undoubtedly the best of the many good things which he did in his life – she said that he should really be named J. G. Club, because of his fondness for these old-fashioned – to some people's minds offensive, because largely all-male – institutions. In many ways, Algy is like one of the Edwardian clubland heroes in the novels by John Buchan and Dornford Yates which he delights in rereading. To say he is clubbable is in one sense an understatement; in another way, though, it would be misleading. Algy Cluff is a shy, retiring person, who is modest about his many achievements. He never chucks his weight about. He is quiet and polite. His most notable characteristic is his humour, and when I think about him, it is always his laugh, and his smiling, amused expression, which come to mind.

Amusement was often displayed on his features when I first met him. He was then the proprietor of the *Spectator*, a magazine of which I was for two happy years the Literary Editor. (The episode is recorded in the following pages!) It was understandable if Algy's amused expression sometimes darkened to exasperation during those years, since his journalists spent his money as if there was no tomorrow, and, as he reveals here, it cost him, in today's terms, a loss of £1.5 million. Thanks to Algy's faith in the magazine, and his preparedness to spend his own money on it, and thanks to the business skills of James Knox, the magazine's publisher, the *Spectator* was saved, and is now a thriving weekly which makes a big profit.

During those years, Algy was a kind host, who entertained me, my wife and my children on innumerable occasions, and, when I parted company with the magazine, continued to be my patron until I was afloat again. This unobtrusive and entirely unnecessary generosity has never been forgotten.

When I first got to know Algy, I was writing about Hilaire Belloc, one of whose more celebrated poems states that 'There's nothing worth the wear of winning / But laughter and the love of friends'. Algy's life bears this out. This book is the opposite of a misery memoir. It rejoices in his kind parents, his good friends and his happy marriage with three splendid sons. His boldness in the field of business and his merriment as a companion have their reward. One of the friends he remembers here with affection was the Man of Letters Peter Quennell, who enjoyed the company of 'our Algy', as he used to call him, especially at White's. Whenever I met Quennell, which was often, he would ask, 'How's our Algy?' We used to agree that our diffident hero was something of a mystery. But now we find the answer to our question in this charming book.

I

Uncertain Start

To reflect on my childhood is a melancholy experience, as paradoxically it could not have been a happier period in my life, blessed as I was with exemplary parents. Being an only child it was a solitary life, but that suited me well.

I was about five when I noticed that in my parents' eyes there was little, if anything, I could do wrong. I was nonetheless put through the rigours of boarding school, firstly at a preparatory school called Mostyn House on the Wirral, owned by a choleric monster called A. M. D. Grenfell. The school is now closed and he is long since dead. The masters were mostly geriatric or eccentric or both.

Life at boarding school had the sole merit for me of enhancing my appreciation of home life. I was never bullied by boys, only by the egregious Grenfell who thrashed me with a cane after I was observed tossing a ball

1

of paper on which I had written the heresy 'Vote Labour' (this must have been the 1950 General Election) at another boy in chapel. Grenfell would probably have been brought in front of the magistrates today. He was followed by his son, Julian, a more gentle soul, now also dead, and the school finally succumbed about two years ago.

I made no enduring friendships there and, although I was Deputy Head Boy of the school, I showed little academic or sporting prowess. However, the school had a well-stocked library with the works of Herman Melville, R. M. Ballantyne, Dornford Yates and Sapper being prominent, and it was in that library that I acquired my lifelong love of books. I was particularly struck and influenced by John Buchan – the only one of those authors whose work is undiminished by time and whom I can read with as much pleasure today. Indeed, his tales of the derring-do of the military and the aristocracy had a strange effect on me. I determined that one day I would be a part of that fantastical world, which indeed I was, although by then I realised it was largely illusory.

The complete absence of privacy – all the dormitories slept at least twenty children – rendered that noun of great importance and an armchair in the school library overlooking the Dee estuary was the nearest I could get to it.

The holidays accordingly were an enchanted period for me, reading or daydreaming in my bedroom, in my father's study or, best of all, in a deckchair in the garden – a glade of willow trees surrounding a small pond where Mrs Street, our housekeeper for many years, would bring me a succession of refreshments. Her tomato sandwiches were incomparable. Food after the War was execrable at the preparatory school but always abundant at home, although my mother managed, I recall, to feed me Bachelors canned ravioli on toast for lunch every day for seven years.

One day at Mostyn House a number of us were instructed to attend the Headmaster's office to meet the legendary J. F. Roxburgh, the founding Headmaster of Stowe School, and so it was that my destiny for the next five years was determined.

❧

I was born in 1940, at which time my parents lived in a handsome house, Mere Dene, overlooking the Mere itself in Cheshire. There was a garden sloping down to the lake with a jetty and a *Swallows and Amazons* dinghy moored alongside. My affection for water and the sea, and immunity from bad weather, was inculcated by the five years I spent on the Dee estuary, and mucking about in that dinghy, although by the time I left for Stowe we had moved to a larger house with a ten-acre garden near Chelford, a small village close to Knutsford.

During the post-War years overseas travel was governed by a limit of £50, as a result of which we chartered a schooner, the *Heatherbell*, based in Falmouth, or cruised on British ships, mostly P & O or Royal Mail Lines, where there was no restriction on sterling expenditure.

My love for things maritime was further developed by many happy holidays on the *Heatherbell*, as was my love for Betty, voluptuous daughter of my father's great friends Bob and Vi Hammond. Bob – large and walrus-moustached – was the genial Managing Director of the *Daily Mail* in the north-west and had kindly printed my first and until now only book, *The Circus and its History*, in 1952 – all of twenty pages long. Most of it was based on a book about circus life given to me by my Aunt Vi and written by Lady Eleanor Smith, aunt of Nicholas Berry who twenty-five years later was to become, and who remains, a close friend.

Of the many cruises we made, the most memorable was on the RMS *Andes* to South America in 1952, visiting São Paulo, Montevideo and Buenos Aires – then in the grip of President Perón. We always lived in some style and ate in a select dining room. I remember being very impressed by the grandeur of our fellow diners, having discerned from the passenger list who they were. They included a Colonel Jack Leslie, his wife and his recently married son Robin. The Colonel was very friendly towards me and, in a curious Anthony Powell fashion, I renewed my acquaintance with him many years later when I became a member of White's Club, of which he was the Chairman. He had won the DSO and MC in the War and was, to me, a very romantic figure.

❧

My father had fought in the First World War in Flanders, as had my maternal grandfather, Freddie, who was badly gassed. Neither of them ever talked of it and would have been greatly surprised at the effusions presently commemorating that horrible and unnecessary calamity. Indeed, I had no idea that my father had seen any military service at all until, during the Second World War, he suddenly materialised wearing the uniform of a Chief Superintendent in the Special Constabulary, with his chest displaying a row of medals. Many of his friends also suddenly revealed by reason of their constabulary work previous gallantry, which would have remained hidden but for this second call to arms.

In particular I remember George H. Smith, my Godfather, a delightful and unassuming

man who turned out to have joined the
Lancashire Fusiliers in 1914, was awarded
the DSO and the MC and was promoted to
Major on the field of battle. I have his photograph on my desk as I write. I had no idea he
had even been in the Army.

There was indeed an absence of any swagger
or exhibition on the part of my father and his
friends, which I believe was due to the horrors
they had endured in the trenches. Sufficient
for them was the luxury of life itself and the
simple pleasures of golf and bridge. My father,
self-deprecating as always, when asked what
his responsibilities as a Chief Superintendent
entailed during the War, said that all he could
recall doing was standing in front of the fruit
machine (then illegal) at the Mere Golf Club
when Lord (Hartley) Shawcross made a visit
to the north-west.

The Mere Golf Club had been founded by
half a dozen local businessmen, including my
father, just before the War. The course was laid
out by James Braid no less, and the professional
was George Duncan, Open Champion in 1920
– a better caricature of a stage Scotsman would
be hard to find. Taciturn and dour, he gave
me my first and only golf lessons and totally
failed to engender in me any enthusiasm for
the game. My father and mother served as
Captains on more than one occasion.

The only swagger was exhibited by another

Godfather, Sir Stanley Holt, who had not served in the War at all, although there was no doubt of his physical courage. Returning home one evening to his huge house in Didsbury, he realised that it was being burgled. He rang 999, seized a poker, searched the house and then the grounds and apprehended a burly figure in a rhododendron bush whom he walloped on the head with the poker, only to discover it was the local policeman.

He was a business partner of my father in a distillery company and no one knew why on earth he had been knighted. His first wife had died and he had a disconcerting habit of placing the box containing her ashes on a chair next to him at the dining-room table. He was even rumoured to have taken her in her box to the Palace Theatre in Manchester where he had reserved two seats … one for him and one for the box. He was the Chairman of the Palace Theatre and he told me that he only had time for professional actors if they called him Sir. I asked him if any of them did, and he conceded the only one was Ken Dodd, who could do no wrong in Sir Stanley's eyes. He had a vast Rolls-Royce and sported a black homburg hat and was very generous to us. In those days all the American musicals would appear at the Palace Theatre before proceeding to London, and we attended the first nights of *Annie Get Your Gun*, *Oklahoma*,

South Pacific and many others. Through the Palace Theatre we became very friendly with Fred Emney, a monocled W. C. Fields (then a famous comedian) lookalike. I was more struck by the beauty of Sally Anne Howes in *Paint Your Wagon*.

လာ

At the instigation of the Headmaster of Mostyn House, my parents were persuaded that Stowe School should be my next destination, largely because of the reputation of J. F. Roxburgh. However, by the time I had secured a place J. F. had permanently retired, allegedly broken by the number of his boys who had been killed in the War, and E. V. Reynolds, another bachelor, had been appointed. Between his appointment and his first term as Headmaster he had, unfortunately for him but also for Stowe, suffered a severe facial accident whilst climbing in Scotland, and the resulting disfigurement rendered him reclusive and abrupt.

My parents and I had personal experience of this when we first met him in his study. We had driven down from Cheshire, a journey that, in those pre-motorway days, took about ten hours with my father at the wheel of his new Bentley. We were ushered into the wintry presence of E. V. Reynolds who said to my father, 'I can give you five minutes.' My father, the most mild-mannered and kindest of men, nearly had a seizure, but by that time it was too late to source another school and the arresting beauty of the place had cast its spell.

So began five more years of schooling, although 'school' was an inaccurate description of Stowe in those days – I used to think 'country club' would have been more appropriate. Remarkably, after our first unsatisfactory interview with Reynolds I never exchanged one word with him for the rest of my time there, except to be chastised after being apprehended smoking a cigar halfway up a cedar tree. Otherwise my life continued in much the same fashion as it had at Mostyn House, without any academic or real sporting achievements to my credit, although my shyness was cured by winning a cross-country race which led to my house, Walpole, securing some cup and my being carried shoulder-high for the first and last time in my life.

The school was, as I subsequently learnt, on the verge of insolvency and bore a rather rundown air. As at Mostyn House, I made few friends. Indeed, it was not until I eventually joined the Army that my capacity for friendship evolved. There were a few exceptions, including Anthony Barbour, known affectionately as Hairy Barbour, being almost entirely covered with it, except on his head. The school published every term what was known as the Blue Book, which contained the names and addresses of the children's parents. It revealed that Barbour lived at Bolesworth Castle, Tattenhall, Cheshire. This we assumed to be a public house for Barbour, although a charming and friendly fellow, looked more Cypriot than aristocrat. Appearances were not deceptive in this case as his father, Major Barbour, had been dispatched on a long overseas tour to cure his penchant for chorus girls and had returned married to a Cypriot lady. However, Bolesworth was indeed a bona fide castle, and I spent some happy days there staying with Anthony. He owned a good 9,000 acres and was a very rich and sound man with a good eye for art, adding works by Malcolm Drummond, Bevan and Augustus John to the Stubbs already in the castle. He married happily, had two daughters, and alas died comparatively young.

Stowe had, like Mostyn House, a motley collection of masters, few of whom, unsurprisingly, had any time for Reynolds. He was finally edged out in favour of Donald Crichton-Miller, the Headmaster of Fettes and, as it turned out, a raving lunatic. The School's reputation was partially restored under the direction of R. Q. Drayson, and two recent headmasters, Jeremy Nicholls and Anthony Wallersteiner, have further enhanced its standing, something of which I have first-hand knowledge, having become a Governor in 1998.

Notwithstanding the lackadaisical manner in which the school was run, I cannot claim to have been in any way unhappy there. Osbert Sitwell stated in his *Who's Who* entry that he was educated in the holidays from Eton. That also applied to me. It was with no regret but with little idea of what to do with myself that I left Stowe in 1958 to study for the Bar.

❡

From the age of sixteen my literary taste had matured and evolved into biography, mostly military and legal. I was enthused by Majoribanks and Colvins' biography of Carson, and F. E. Smith, Marshall Hall, Patrick Hastings and Rufus Isaacs I regarded with awe.

By this time my father's wine shipping and importing business had flourished and he had also built up a chain of off-licences known as Empire Wine Stores, for much of his stock came from South Africa. It was clear that he cherished the hope that I would enter the family business at its headquarters in Manchester. Nothing could have been further removed from my own aspirations, and when I advised my parents that I was a Lord Chancellor in the making they typically supported what turned out to be a short-lived plan.

I was registered with the Middle Temple and began to eat my dinners, as was the requirement in those days. My father found me a one-room apartment in Sloane Gardens and I had two suits made at his tailors, Johns & Pegg. I knew no one in London except Captain Clarence French, a nephew of the Field Marshal and down on his luck, whom my father took pity on and to whom he paid a retainer, primarily I imagined to keep an eye on me. Charming though he was, all I can recall him doing was introducing me to the pleasures of alcohol and so my studies in Chancery Lane ground to a halt.

I joined the Lansdowne Club, the first of many, which in those days bore some resemblance to P. G. Wodehouse's Drones Club. Clubs have, as will be apparent, played a large part in my life. They used to provide a harmless refuge for the male of the species, but thanks to the new dispensation, that obtains no more. My wife found my direct debit list once and suggested I change my name from Cluff to Club, as I spent so much money on and in them. One certainly needs two clubs – one to repair to if you are feeling cheerful and gregarious, and the other to repair to if you are feeling curmudgeonly and wish to be alone. Dinner alone, with a good book and a good bottle of wine and a good waiter, is a necessary palliative from time to time. My favourite London clubs are White's, Brooks's, The Travellers and Pratt's. Of this last I am an Honorary Member, a result of Andrew, the old Duke of Devonshire and proprietor of Pratt's, attending our wedding in Hong Kong. 'What would you like as a wedding present?' he courteously asked my wife and me after the ceremony. Neither of us could think of anything until he said, 'Would you like to be a member of Pratt's?'

'Oh thank you,' my wife replied, never having heard of it and not realising until too late that it is one of the few remaining all-male clubs. I am also a member of the Royal Yacht Squadron, where I have the privilege of being the Honorary Librarian, and I have recently been invited to be an Honorary Member of the Chelsea Arts Club, an unexpected and welcome compliment.

In 1958 I had enlisted in the Inns of Court Regiment and my military enthusiasm led me to conclude that it was a Guards officer that I really wanted to be. My decision, typically supported by my long-suffering parents, was the right one in the sense that I never for a moment regretted a day of the six years spent in the Army and I became, perhaps disproportionately when I view my relatively undistinguished military career, very proud of being an officer in the Grenadier Guards.

2

ARMY – WEST AFRICA

Clarence French endorsed my military aspirations and introduced me to
Colonel Hanmer (Pat) Hanbury in the latter's
flat in Eaton Square. Hanbury was a retired
Grenadier and after he had recovered from
the sartorial solecism I had committed by
wearing a British Warm overcoat (decidedly
non-U, he advised me), he agreed to arrange
for me to be interviewed at the Regimental
Headquarters in Birdcage Walk.

At that time, 1959, the Grenadiers had
three Battalions and the so-called Regimental
Lieutenant-Colonel was a full Colonel. This
was Alex Gregory-Hood, an exotic figure,
chauffeur-driven in a Jensen by his soldier
servant (as we called them then). He had
had a good War and was to become an art
dealer of some distinction and imagination.
Curiously, his daughter is married to a former
member of my current board of directors,

Brian FitzGerald. He accepted me as a candidate for a Short Service Commission and I was instructed to present myself on 20th June at Aldershot Barracks.

As it happened one of my friends from the Lansdowne Club, Nicholas Freeman, was to have his twenty-first birthday party at his parents' house in Chichester on 19th June. I resolved to attend the party, and then drive from Chichester to Aldershot in the early hours of the morning in my car, a Sunbeam Alpine, of which I was very proud. My mother had given it to me as a joining-up present to cheer me up as I was developing some anxiety about whether I would be able to cope with the rigour of Army life.

The party proceeded and I managed to detach myself from the beguiling charms of a tall blonde and set off for Aldershot. I had only the haziest idea of where Aldershot was and what I was going to do when I got there, which I finally did at 4 a.m. I located a car park adjacent to Mons Barracks, staggered into a barrack room in my dinner jacket, found an empty bed and passed out. The next thing I knew I was being bawled at by an infuriated Coldstream Drill Sergeant. It appeared that the 'car park' was in fact the drill square and all the new entrants were formed up around my car.

ↄ

The commander of our Cadet Wing was an amazing figure named Major Sir Torquil Matheson ('Bart'), who was rumoured to call his wife 'Wife'. He was an impressive figure, but no intellectual and used to go puce in the face when concentrating on something complicated like the leave roster. I was summoned to his presence later that day.

'You have a car, Cluff, I gather,' he said, as if I had some appalling disease. 'A car is a thoroughly bad influence on you and your fellow cadets and I am confiscating it! Give me the keys.' In those days there were separate keys for the ignition and the boot. I gave him the keys for the boot, which, as far as I know, he still has.

I then felt the full force of military training life – rigours that would be unacceptable today, but were strangely uplifting then.

The first event was an introduction to the course by CSM Thomas, a Grenadier, and the most terrifying man I had ever come across. He was underneath the bluster the most kindly man, and high on the list of my personal achievements was earning his approval, which he eventually disclosed at Sennybridge Battle Camp six months later.

It was a particularly hot summer, and the combination of the heat and the exhaustion involved in being paraded and bawled at by tough non-commissioned Guards officers produced the oddly intoxicating consequence of humour. We laughed so much that it began to hurt. I shared a barrack room with a horde of other cadets (I think I was the only Guardsman). Two of them, John Edwards, Intelligence Corps, and Michael Haines, Rifle Brigade, were in a section called 4B, or 'fabulous four B' as we called it. Edwards eventually joined ITN and Haines became a distinguished accountant. They were both highly intelligent and I owe them a lot. Haines, alas now dead, produced an extraordinary volume of autobiography, fortunately privately printed, revealing himself to be of a seriously melancholic and bitter disposition behind all the gaiety.

As the course proceeded Sergeants Gulstan (Coldstream Guards), Fawcett (Irish Guards) and Licquorish (Grenadier Guards) gradually became our firm friends and it was with some sadness that we bade them farewell after our Passing Out Parade in Aldershot, in the presence of the town Mayor and other dignitaries. We were formed up outside the Cathedral and I was chatting to Michael Haines. 'Cluff and 'aines, stop ruddy talking and get in that fucking Cathedral!' were the immortal words of Sergeant Fawcett, which reverberated up and down the nave.

I was gazetted to the 3rd Battalion of the Grenadiers, commanded by another charming War hero, Tony Way. We were stationed at Wellington Barracks, and for some months conducted public guard duties including the Trooping of the Colour in 1960 for which, to my horror, I was selected as Ensign to the Colour, which is the star role of the Trooping ceremony. This was something of an ordeal, but definitely ranks as one of my proudest moments. In November 2013 I went to a dinner for all the officers who had carried their Regimental Colours on the Trooping during the reign of HM the Queen, attended by virtually every Ensign since her accession, at which I had the honour of sitting next to the Queen.

When stationed at Wellington Barracks I became very friendly with Jasper Larken, the son of Wyatt, a Naval Captain, and the grandson of an Admiral. Jasper and I teamed up with my closest friend at the time, Johnnie Pascoe, who was in the Scots Guards, and bought a yacht, *Linette*. She was an elegant ketch and around, on and beneath her we had the happiest and merriest days I can recall, quite often spent at angles between 45 and 90 degrees on most of the available mud banks on the South Coast. Every weekend we drove down to the Hamble River and either stayed aboard *Linette* or at the Royal Southern Yacht Club. Johnnie, an Etonian and a most attractive and cheerful character, boasted a beautiful and charming if silent girlfriend, Veronica MacQueen, who maintained some order when we were aboard *Linette*. The

Royal Southern in those days was a very cosy small club and there was a restaurant, the Lobster Pot, at which we spent an inordinate amount of time, always dining there before driving back to London and the Army on Sunday evenings.

A leading personality around the Hamble River then was Bruce Campbell, a fellow Royal Southern member and power-boat enthusiast. Tiring of *Linette*, we decided to acquire a power boat, *Rouge et Noir*. By this time I had joined the Guards Parachute Company at Pirbright, Jasper had left for New York and the life of a stockbroker and Johnnie, ahead of his time, had joined the computer pioneer ICL. He duly and wisely married Veronica. Both he and Jasper alas died too young. When I was posted to Cyprus, being by this time the sole proprietor of *Rouge et Noir*, I asked Bruce to find a buyer for her. Bruce's son, Michael, became a successful businessman and the Commodore of the Royal Yacht Squadron and, together with the present Commodore, Christopher Sharples, played a prominent part in sustaining that Club's preeminent position.

છે

The Army, now too small, was then arguably too large and recruiting became a challenge. Inevitably the 3rd Battalion was disbanded, and I have a photograph of myself and a fellow officer marching the Colours into the Guards Chapel where they now rest.

I was then posted to the 1st Battalion, which was stationed at Kandahar Barracks in Tidworth. The Battalion was commanded by Lt.-Colonel David Fraser, popularly known, although not to his face, as 'the Razor'. Of Scottish aristocratic lineage, he was an intellectual soldier of considerable consequence, although lacking in what are now known as 'people skills'. He eventually became a full General and a military historian of distinction, and wrote an engaging autobiography. His first wife, unusually in those days, left him for another woman. I was exceptionally fond of him while taking no liberties.

The other Battalion officers were a most interesting and entertaining group, almost all of whom were to become lifelong friends of mine. They included a number of national service officers who had had their military service deferred whilst they attended university, and they were stimulating company. Prominent among them were John (Cats' Eyes) Semple and James Cheetham. Semple's fey behaviour caused some comment. On completion of a short course into the mysteries of the sub-machine gun we were all required to deliver a short lecture. When Semple's turn came he picked up his gun gingerly and declared: 'This is the baby machine gun – oh fuck it's covered in oil!'

Semple became an amateur archaeologist and used to write me amusing letters from a dig in Egypt, improbably called Kasr-el-Wizz. He always signed them 'Yours until the Last Trump Sounds'. Cheetham, handsome, clever and laid-back, ironically became a rich man as a result of his spasmodic exertions as a Discount Broker in the City, and subsequently by backing his brother Anthony's publishing businesses.

My first alarming experience of the Razor arose as a result of the Duty Officer being required to sleep in a camp bed in the Commanding Officer's office. It was my turn and I awoke, opened my eyes and to my horror discerned a pair of highly polished boots six inches from my face. They encased the Razor's legs. I looked at my watch, which registered the time as 8 a.m., rather than the 6 a.m. I should have awoken. I accordingly had the uncomfortable experience of getting up and dressed before the basilisk glare of the Razor. 'You imbecile,' he intoned, 'you will do a further period of Duty Officer again tonight.'

That evening I went to sleep, having set my alarm for 5 a.m., when at about midnight the telephone rang. I picked it up and a voice said, 'This is Charing Cross Police Station. Do you have a Major X in your Battalion?'

'Yes,' I said. 'Is he all right?'

'He is under arrest for persistently importuning a plain-clothes officer for immoral purposes.'

Heavens, I thought. Last night had been bad enough, but to wake the Razor with this news was, to say the least, not going to be popular. However, that is what I had to do. I then witnessed a procedure of ruthless efficiency, which provided for the unfortunate Major to have not only retired from the Army before he appeared before the Magistrates the next morning, but also to have secured employment as a security officer for a diamond mine in Sierra Leone. I have often wondered what became of that unfortunate officer, who fell foul of one of the most unsavoury policing policies of the time.

જીજી

In 1961 we were advised that we were to embark on the troopship *Devonshire* for the British Cameroons in West Africa, a country of which few of the officers and none of the Guardsmen had heard. Before the First World War the Cameroons had been a German colony and was divided between Britain and France after the Armistice. The lion's share was awarded to France. The British section comprised a narrow strip ranging from coastal swamp country to an escarpment – two hundred metres inland

– revealed magnificent mountainous country suitable for cattle grazing.

The central part of the country seemed barren, other than some banana plantations owned by Elders & Fyffe's. The coastal strip, including the volcano Mount Cameroon, had a small port at Victoria and the administrative capital Buea. The United Nations had determined that the British Cameroons was too small to qualify for independence. Instead they were to be offered the choice of merging with the French Cameroons (and accordingly changing their entire legal system, language, currency etc) or merging with Nigeria. Incredibly they voted in a plebiscite to merge with the French sector. The 1st Battalion Grenadier Guards were to be there to ensure peace before the plebiscite.

The voyage out on the *Devonshire* was the last by any troopship. The Bibby Line were the owners and, curiously, it was run by the RAF Transport Command. We officers, about thirty of us, had roughly two thirds of the accommodation, which it occurred to me might cause some trouble. In an unfortunate fit of exuberance, we tossed various items of first-class furniture into the Bay of Biscay and a significant proportion of our pay was redirected to the Bibby Line as a result. We were allowed off the ship at Las Palmas, and because a number of officers and Guardsmen were late back on board, it was decided by the

Razor that at the next and last stop, Lagos, none would be permitted to land. The men were philosophical about this, until a tender was observed containing the Razor himself in mess dress, setting off, as it subsequently emerged, to have dinner with the High Commissioner Anthony Head, and his wife, known as Dot. The Guardsmen were enraged by this insensitive display, as indeed were some of the livelier officers.

Nicholas Villiers, James Cheetham, Jasper Larken and I resolved to follow the Razor's example and acquired the use of a banana boat for ten shillings and set off for a last night in 'civilisation' with 'Pips' Royston, Head's ADC. It was the next morning before we reboarded the *Devonshire*, leading to a late departure and considerable displeasure from the Razor.

Arriving in the Cameroons, we were given separate sections of the country to manage. The Queen's Company, commanded by Philip Haslett, a charming, bald, moustachioed Major, whom I thought of as being as old as Methuselah (but who was probably no more than thirty-five) was given the northern part of the country, based on a market town called Bamenda, inevitably known as Bumenda. Number 2 company, commanded by the delightful and intelligent Irishman Nick Hales-Pakenham-Mahon (known as 'Hail Shining Morn' by the Guardsmen), controlled the central part of the country based at Mamfe, which was below sea level and very unhealthy. The rest, together with the Razor and the HQ Company, remained in Buea. The Razor seems to have been seldom seen, most of his work being conducted by the incomparable Peter Thwaites, an amateur playwright, and the two Quartermasters, Lou Drouet and Dick Dickinson. Thwaites dashed off a ditty to celebrate our magnificent Irish nurse Maureen Noonan, which as I recall read: 'Maureen noon and night / Loud the jungle drums are drumming / Is it true that Matron's coming?' We also irreverently submitted an entry for a lyric for the new National Anthem along the lines of 'We are independent but we don't know why' to the refrain, 'Have a banana!', their sole export.

I, to my joy, was suddenly detached from the Battalion and, with a Drill Sergeant and various NCOs, charged with the task of training the new Mobile Police Force in Jakiri, a hill station miles away from anywhere. I was provided with my own bungalow, and settled down in that heavenly setting overlooking the Bamboutos Mountains.

The Police were mobile in the sense that they had feet, but little else, and Drill Sergeant Jeffries, Sergeant Cattle and I set out to make Guardsmen of them. I had little to do, which suited me fine. I ordered six books a month from Hatchards in Piccadilly, which miraculously found their way to Jakiri (most of them I still have). My mother sent me a wind-up gramophone with three records: *The Sound of Music*, 'All Aboard for Margate' and 'The Massed Bands of the Brigade of Guards', which, together with a recording of the Cuban band the Lecuona Boys given me by Nicholas Villiers, I played ad nauseam, prompting the visiting Senior Major, Paul Freyberg (son of the Field Marshal), to threaten to confiscate them.

I had a cook to myself who introduced himself as Alexander Wanka. 'I can't have a cook called Wanka!' I told him. He shrugged, reappeared the following day and announced that he had changed his name to 'Any Where Wednesday', which seemed a bit drastic, but 'Wednesday' he remained.

One day my life changed. I was sitting on the veranda, doubtless reading a book from Hatchards and listening with rapt pleasure to 'All Aboard for Margate', when there appeared a curious procession at the steps of my bungalow. It was led by an elderly gentleman wearing a top hat, a mackintosh and nothing else, as became apparent when he stopped to relieve himself before advancing up the steps. This was my first meeting with the 'Fon of Banso', the Paramount Chief of the area. He was a most loveable gentleman; we became firm friends and from that moment on we went hunting or carousing together virtually every day. He lived in a sort of palace known as the Fon's Takibu, in the centre of a compound that housed his innumerable wives and bodyguards.

Shortly after I met him a letter was delivered from the Takibu addressed to Major General Cluff of the Grenadier Guards. This was accelerated promotion, considering I was a twenty-year-old Second Lieutenant. The first lines read, 'I am in the shameful position of having 120 sons and not one of them is in the Grandeur Guards. What are you going to do about it?' The letter was signed with a thumbprint beneath the legend 'I am, yes, The Fon of Banso!!' I thought this a very elegant way of signing off. The next letter I had to address to the bank manager in Aldershot, concerning my £50 overdraft, I signed 'I am, yes, Second Lieutenant Cluff'. Alas this produced no discernible improvement in my relationship with the Midland Bank.

When this idyllic period was over, and the Mobile Police Force had been turned into an immaculate unit thanks to the skills of the Drill Sergeants, the time came to return to the coast and the *Devonshire*. The Fon was upset by my impending departure, as was I, and commanded all his people to attend a party in the Takibu compound. He sat on a large throne, myself on a smaller one, both of us taking occasional swigs from some dubious bottle of rice wine. In front of us there gyrated large numbers of nubile and naked girls. I knew what was coming when, after a while, the Fon leant over and enquired whether there was anything I wanted. I mumbled incoherently, the dancing stopped and he gave some instructions. After a few minutes six young men appeared, towing behind them the biggest lady I had ever seen in Africa, the Fon's notion of absolute beauty. The Fon leered at me and smiled. 'Sorry, Fon,' I said, 'I have suddenly got a shocking headache.'

And I sheepishly returned to my bungalow for my final solitary night.

3

ARMY – BORNEO

We duly re-embarked on the troopship *Devonshire*, having successfully discharged our task of monitoring law and order prior to the UN plebiscite with only one Guardsman fatality, resulting from a clash with the Bamileke tribe who sporadically arrived from the French Cameroons across the river with the intention of disrupting life. Our arrival at Southampton was delayed by bad weather in the Bay of Biscay and we arrived in the middle of the night to discover that the 'heroes return' celebrations had been cancelled.

Back in Kandahar Barracks I experienced a rush of blood to the head and resolved to apply to join the Guards (Independent) Parachute Company, an elite unit of about a hundred personnel, drawn from all of the Guards regiments and subject only to their surviving a two-week endurance test in the

Brecon Beacons. This reduced me to physical rubble, although there was worse to come.

My parachute training took place at RAF Benson. Great care was taken to ensure that we were properly prepared. The course lasted two weeks and built up from jumping off platforms in an aircraft hangar to two rather chilling jumps through a trap door beneath a tethered balloon and culminating with six aerial jumps, the last of which was conducted at night. 'Jumping from nothing into bugger all' was how it was described by the Guardsmen, and it was rather alarming hurtling towards the ground, which became impossible to discern the nearer it got. The only casualty we suffered, however, was someone who managed to break his ankle getting into the bus after we had finished.

I was staying in some comfort in the RAF Officers' Mess and, the night we completed our final jump, I decided to have a bath whilst watching my portable TV before alerting my friends to my achievement. It was whilst having that bath that I saw on TV the assassination of President Kennedy. I kept my counsel as I dined alone in the Officers' Mess that melancholy evening.

I was accepted by the Parachute Company, having previously also passed the Regular Commissions Board. I was appointed Captain and joined the Company at Pirbright. The other troop commanders included a kindly

Coldstreamer, Philip Fazil, who shortly after lost a leg to a landmine in Aden and Patrick Beresford, the Intelligence Officer and a highly competent soldier, who became and remains a close friend, as did his brother, Tyrone Waterford. The company was commanded by an obnoxious Irish Guards Major.

∞

Towards the end of 1963 the situation on the troubled island of Cyprus took another turn for the worse and, as we set off for the Christmas holidays, we were warned that should we receive a telegram reading 'Barclays Bank' we were to return at once to RAF Benson, where I had done my parachute training. I drove the entire pre-motorway distance home to my parents and, as I parked my car in front of the house, my mother rushed out in great excitement: 'Darling there is a telegram for you!'

I read the dreaded words: 'Barclays Bank'. I swore, had a cup of tea and drove all the way back to Oxfordshire.

The Guards Parachute Company was the Pathfinder Company of the Parachute Brigade and it was accordingly our task to arrive at the destination first. However, I was in an RAF Beverly plane of Transport Command, carrying three Ferret Scout cars and a handful of Guardsmen, that elected to develop engine trouble, grounding us in Nice, Malta and El Adem in Libya. We finally arrived some days after the last Royal Army Pay Corps personnel! No one seemed to notice.

There followed a period of some unpleasant soldiering, where our primary duty was the protection of the outnumbered Turkish Cypriots from their Greek enemies. This involved us in breaking the blockades erected on the roads to prevent food being supplied to Turkish villages. We were left in no doubt by the Greeks as to their dislike for us, and it was their view that our sympathy was with the Turks. In this surmise they were correct.

Curiously, in November 2013 I returned to Cyprus fifty years on as the Hon. Colonel of the 3rd Battalion The Princess of Wales's Royal Regiment, who were patrolling the Green Line as part of the United Nations Force. It is scarcely credible that this line is still being policed at such enormous cost. Here I committed a solecism. By 2013 there were female officers whose charms were concealed by baggy combat uniforms. One evening the United Nations Senior Officer kindly gave a cocktail party at his residence. I spotted an attractive blonde lady and enquired whether she was married to an officer. 'No,' she said, 'I am an officer and what is more I sat next to you at lunch today!'

 భ

Whilst the Company was in Cyprus, the SAS regiment had experienced a number of casualties, particularly of officers, some of whom had been beheaded in the Yemen. The belligerent President Sukarno of Indonesia, in his political death throes, had then invaded Malaysian Borneo. The dense jungle bordering Malaysia and Indonesia could only sensibly be policed by specially trained forces. The decision was taken to offer the Guards Parachute Company to the SAS as a new squadron, to be known as 'G' squadron. This, to my horror, involved another round of endurance tests in the Brecon Beacons and, this time, a further period of torture in the jungle near Ipoh in Malaya.

Although I have strong legs and the capacity to cover long distances, I have poor physical strength and it is a total mystery how I managed to survive that SAS training. But survive it I did, sustained mostly by a sense of humour.

When we had completed our training, we embarked on a ship from Singapore to Sibu in Borneo. From there we were conveyed by launch to Nanga Gaat in the Third Division of Sarawak. From there we were landed in the jungle by Wessex helicopters. The squadron was divided into discrete groups of four – an officer, a medic, a wireless operator and a linguist. Our sole communication with the outside world was in Morse code. Everything we needed we carried on our backs. We slept in hammocks fashioned from parachute cloth and slung between two suitable trees. Determining the health of these trees was important, as occasional gales swept through the jungle and one could hear sustained crashes as the weaker trees were uprooted. Having organised our accommodation we then cleared an area of jungle large enough to admit helicopters, should we require reinforcing. Then we patrolled the river crossings to watch out for any evidence of incursion by the Indonesian Army.

For the first few days we all jumped six inches in the air whenever a twig snapped, but we quickly realised the unlikelihood of anyone being so stupid as to be where we were. We were fed by air every two weeks, marking our location by raising an orange helium balloon above the tree line which the RAF would identify and parachute containers of food to us. These containers always seemed to hold a tin of Australian stew, curry powder, an oatmeal biscuit and some Kraft cheese. We were constantly hungry.

My mother again entered the scene. Concerned that I was not getting enough to eat and having only the vaguest notion of where Borneo was (somewhere near the Isle of Wight I think she thought), she instructed Fortnum & Mason to send hampers of food to Sibu. Fortnum's duly carried out these unusual instructions and the hampers, unknown to me, began piling up in Sibu. This caused great hilarity amongst the RAF and, on one supply drop, they included a hamper. Typically, its parachute failed to open and we mournfully scraped foie gras off palm fronds and were violently sick. This incident was recorded on Jack De Manio's BBC morning report.

One morning an event occurred which changed the lives of our small group. As I have said, we slept in hammocks made out of our parachutes and, provided you smeared the rope with a repellent to prevent the loathsome leeches attaching themselves to you whilst asleep, they were reasonably comfortable. We had placed our hammocks around the clearing we had made to admit helicopters in the event of our being attacked. We used to wake at dawn and cook what passed for breakfast with a blanket around our shoulders, for this part of Sarawak was mountainous and chilly as the sun seldom penetrated through the tree canopy.

On this morning I was immediately conscious of a strong odour, followed by a shock realisation that we were surrounded by what first appeared to be thousands, but in reality was about fifty, tribesmen. They were an alarming sight – covered in blue dye, with long black hair and no teeth (they fell out as the result of some vitamin deficiency when they were teenagers). All were carrying spears. This looks tricky, I thought, as I looked over to see if Field, our excellent and imperturbable Irish Guards Wireless Operator, was contacting Sibu.

In the event, no action was required as it rapidly became evident that they were more scared of us than we were of them. Their self-appointed leader, Ninyang, made various signs suggestive of goodwill and our linguist Guardsman Handley (later a Lieutenant Colonel) began a sort of dialogue in halting Malay. These people were part of what the anthropologists call a 'hunter/gatherer' tribe, known as Punans. To our mild embarrassment it emerged that they had been shadowing us for some days without our noticing, so good was their forest work. They were part of a larger group of about a hundred and fifty individuals who roamed around the region along the Sungai (river) Danum. Their primary food came from the felling of sago trees and their location was governed by the supply of those trees. They also hunted animals using blowpipes with darts, which had a form of strychnine on the point and caused a temporary paralysis of the nervous system of the prey, mostly monkeys.

This jungle meeting could not have suited us better. It appeared that they, timid and primitive, had been from time to time used as forced labour by the Indonesians when they had lived in Kalimantan (Indonesian Borneo), so they had fled across the border into Sarawak to evade their tormentors. Instead of the four of us we were now a further one hundred and fifty in strength and they willingly acted as both our eyes and ears. Our co-existence could not have been more appropriate to both of our purposes. The only downside was the putrid smell which emanated from their prey and we had to ensure we hung our parachute beds upwind of the Punan camp. They seemed to be an entirely harmonious community, which operated by a form of common consent. I regret that we accelerated their arrival into the twentieth century as, along with our food supplies, we began receiving surplus amounts of salt and sugar for their consumption. I detected growing evidence of disputes occurring over the division of spoils.

Doubtless owing to the prodigious amounts of bromide in our diet, their womenfolk held no attraction for us. However, they were chain smokers and I occasionally accepted their offer each evening of a cigarette. I never smoked cigarettes but enjoyed cigars or a pipe, both of which were banned in the jungle. When I left the Army the following year and, back in the UK, attended my first party in what was then 'swinging London', I became aware of a familiar acrid odour. I realised that I had been regularly smoking marijuana on Her

Majesty's Service without having the faintest notion of what it was.

ↀ

Some years after our departure the hapless Punans were apparently forcibly resettled in coastal regions, with many unfortunate repercussions. This included the detention and execution of Nanyang, a young warrior, who had been put to work with a logging company. He ran amok and murdered a number of his alien co-workers. Not able to speak any recognised language, he was nonetheless put through the judicial process with the death sentence resulting.

Indonesia finally gave up the war, known as 'Confrontation' by the Malaysians. Alas, subsequently large swathes of the forest in Sarawak in which we lived have now been culled of their grand trees by ruthless Chinese lumber companies.

This was the conclusion, in 1965, of my military career, for I felt ready for change and was more than conscious of my military limitations, in particular a tendency not to do what I had been told to do. A touching moment occurred when we were back in Sibu. The unpleasant Major who commanded the company and of whom, through being in the jungle, I had happily seen nothing, came up to me in a kind of faux-friendly manner and invited me to go for a walk with him. After about 200 yards of silence he stopped and said: 'You don't like me do you!'

'As a matter of fact I can't stand the sight of you,' I replied.

ఴ

On our way back to the UK we spent some time at Nee Soon Barracks in Singapore, the scene of another notable event in my young life. Being strictly speaking on leave, I liberated myself from Nee Soon Barracks and sought some much-needed comfort by staying at The Goodwood Park Hotel, a building which had been the German Embassy before a skilful conversion into a hotel by a Chinese businessman, Khoo Teck Puat, of whom more later.

I had been given an introduction to Alec Adams, the Political Advisor to the Commander-in-Chief of the Far East Land Forces, and duly made contact with him. Many years later I was to give the address at his funeral. Alec had spent most of his Foreign Office career in Thailand and in 1945 he came to know two quite different, but equally remarkable and admirable, characters through their work in Special Operations. These were Ben Hervey-Bathhurst, a Major in the Grenadier Guards who looked every inch the part, and Charles Letts, who had worked for Jardine Waugh in Singapore, been captured when the island was invaded in December 1941, and imprisoned in Thailand until 1945. He spoke Thai, had enormous physical strength and courage and was credited by many with saving their lives by conducting a black market in medical supplies. This involved escapades the other side of the wire when, risking his life, he was able to satisfy the need for medical supplies while also satisfying his other need – young Thai ladies. There was a suggestion in the obituary notice that there had been a touch of fantasy in some of his claims. However, at a dinner at The Travellers Club twenty-five years ago, Sir Denis White, a fellow inmate in the Thai camp, told me that he would not have survived had it not been for Charles' bravery.

Ben Hervey-Bathurst returned to Eastnor Castle in Herefordshire, having married into the Somers-Cocks family, the proprietors there, and the estate is now admirably managed by his two sons James and George. Curiously, another coincidence arose when I was the proprietor of *Apollo* magazine many years later and I appointed Anna Somers-Cocks as the Editor in succession to Denys Sutton.

Alec Adams gave me a warm welcome over dinner in his wonderful Colonial villa and introduced me to Charles Letts, who had returned after captivity to Jardines. Letts had been in the Far East since 1937. He was tall and well-built, with black hair and a strong facial cast. He had never married, although he was an incorrigible womaniser and possessed a lethal stamina that left men half his age in awe. We became firm friends that night. He had accumulated a number of directorships of rubber and tin mining companies, primarily through his association with a grim Chinese, Lee Loy Seng. His career with Jardines had recently ended rather mysteriously; I think he felt that he should have been appointed the Taipan in Hong Kong, whereas the much younger Henry Keswick, scion of the family, had been correctly preferred. He advised me that rubber and palm oil plantation companies were nearly all British-controlled and listed on the London Stock Exchange and, in his view, the London investors had failed to spot the potential value in these estates. He explained that they were valued on a multiple of their relatively modest earnings, whereas in reality they were property companies occupying real estate around the metropolitan conurbations in Malaysia.

Since Malaysia's economy was growing fast, the cities would necessarily expand through plantation land. Notwithstanding my zero commercial experience, I judged that this made a lot of sense and I passed it all on to my father who had just sold the family business to Ind Coope and Allsopp (later to become

Allied Breweries). My father invested heavily and very profitably in many of these plantation companies, and whenever he sold at a profit he gave that profit to me. This process began almost immediately and I felt rather light-headed as large amounts of cash began appearing in my Midland Bank account.

I had flown back to the UK from Singapore and returned to the Guards Depot prior to my retirement. My parents, as thoughtful as ever, drove down to the Depot from Cheshire, my father in the Bentley and my mother in another much more modest car, a Ford I think. The plan being that they would leave the Ford for me so that I would have immediate use of a car on my return. According to my father, when they arrived at the Officers' Mess the Mess Sergeant made as if to get into the Bentley, only to be told that it was the Ford that was being delivered.

'The Captain won't like that, Sir,' the Sergeant observed.

My father's reply was, I believe, colourful.

The final episode of my military career concerned my leaving present. Silver statuettes of Guards Parachute Company Guardsmen had been cast, set on Connemara marble bases and were available for £100 each. My Troop Sergeant, Jamieson, said the men would like me to have one. I was touched by this, until I realised that as the whip-round had raised a mere £3.50 I was obliged to pay the balance myself. However, the memento now sits proudly on my dining-room table.

⌘

At this time, I used some of my plantation cash to acquire a small but very successful bookshop which sold or rented books by the yard. A sort of anti-culture business. It was the creation of the two bright and beautiful daughters, Ros and Toni, of Jack Clifford Wolff, war hero and then a well-known commodity broker and Sunningdale Golf Club stalwart. The shop was to be found in Orange Square, which defined its unusual name, The Square Orange Bookshop. Our customers were chiefly interior decorators, anxious to convey some faux impression of culture on behalf of their clients. By reason of our friendship with the zany Christie's book specialist, Major Bill Spowers, we also did a good trade selling off the attractively-bound dross from the important libraries that were disposed of by Christie's.

Bill was an interesting character – small, wiry, dapper, well-connected and Australian. In the War he had joined the Parachute Regiment and was serving in Italy in 1943 when occured a rather odd incident that nearly brought an end to his career with a court martial. His father, a much-decorated Colonel, was locked in a prisoner of war camp close by Bill's Battalion. Bill was ordered to go on a night patrol to reconnoitre German positions prior to an attack the following day, and he asked the soldiers in his patrol if they would instead try to trigger his father's escape. They agreed and, reaching the camp perimeter wire, somehow made contact with Spowers Senior, who although much moved by his son's extraordinary filial devotion, urged young Bill to call it off and return to his lines. Tragically, while doing so they were ambushed with loss of life. Bill was spared the court martial and went on to become a celebrated eccentric, once driving his Rolls-Royce from Morocco to India via Egypt. He also owned a fire engine garaged at his estate near Windlesham, together with a bulldozer for a massive landscape gardening programme, which has eventually evolved into an important arboretum.

The Square Orange Bookshop prospered, but the beauty of its staff rendered early wedlock for them inevitable. Ros married John Wallinger, a partner in my brokers Panmure Gordon, and they remain happily together fifty years later. Toni wed a prosperous businessman, David Parkes, although that marriage did not succeed. Perhaps I should have married one of them myself, because that was the end of The Square Orange Bookshop.

4

London – The City

My father's generosity, doubtless misguided, removed the imperative for me to earn my living, and so I was gliding about during 1966 when I became associated, I can hardly call it employment, with an organisation called the Ionian Bank and so spent half of that year lotus-eating in New York on their behalf.

Towards the end of 1965, I had been adopted by Ardwick Conservative Association as their Parliamentary candidate. The Chairman was an irascible solicitor, Walter Lyon, with whom I established an uneasy working relationship. The seat was rock-solid Labour and the sitting member was Leslie Lever, the elder brother of Harold Lever who represented the neighbouring constituency of Cheetham Hill, and who was appointed Financial Secretary to the Treasury by Harold Wilson.

Both were solicitors. Leslie was an amazing

figure, so awful that I quite liked him. Irrepressible as he was, he boasted a Papal decoration, even though he was an Orthodox Jew. When I rose to speak at a public meeting he disarmingly led the applause, and then suggested in his speech that the Conservative Party should find me a safe seat 'somewhere else'. In fact I had been adopted without being on the Conservative Party's official list of candidates, so that was most unlikely. Harold Lever married Diana, a very rich and charming Lebanese lady. During the period of exchange control when UK citizens were restricted to £50 expenditure whilst overseas, Harold was observed in Gstaad playing backgammon for £50 a point.

My own politics were those of the Romantic Tory and my interests were confined to defence and foreign affairs. I established some kudos by visiting South Vietnam, about which I wrote mostly for *The Statist*, a magazine that ceased publication shortly afterwards. So I addressed the bemused and uninterested folk of Ardwick with endless speeches about events in the Far East. I contested the 1966 General Election but made little impression on Leslie's majority.

എ

Meanwhile, I had begun to increase my social mobility. This was largely achieved by sharing a flat, 42 Wilton Place (now the Berkeley), with Army friends Brian Alexander (son of the Field Marshal), Nicholas Villiers, Patrick Lichfield, Andrew Parker-Bowles and Donough O'Brien, all ex-Guards officers.

I also joined the St James's Club, located in a beautiful building at 106 Piccadilly. The dining room, overlooking Green Park, had a ceiling painted by Angelica Kaufmann. In that lovely room I enjoyed many a dinner, on occasions sharing the room with Osbert Sitwell and Evelyn Waugh (complete with ear trumpet). Evelyn Waugh often dined there with his publisher, Jack Macdougall, a renowned trencherman and better known as the father of Mary (now Mrs Ian Dunlop), a lovely bluestocking who broke a number of hearts. Jack was the recipient of a telegram from Waugh who had been advised that an American academic, one Professor Stopp, was threatening to write a book about him. 'STOP STOPP STOP' read the telegram (in those days, the word 'stop' was used as punctuation).

The club staff were as dotty as many of the members, of whom the most celebrated was Bert, the then Duke of Marlborough. He lunched there every day, and every day a fellow member known as Loopy Whitbread endeavoured to sit next to him. 'Fuck off Loopy' were the only words I heard His Grace utter, although he delivered himself of a witty response when, having dropped a sixpence in the hall, he was waiting for Paddy, the hall porter, to pick it up. Paddy showed no such inclination, moving His Grace to order him to do so.

'It's only a sixpence, Your Grace,' protested Paddy.

'It might be only a sixpence to you,' he retorted, 'but it's 19/6 to me.' Those were the days when tax was virtually 100 per cent of income.

Many of the members had been reduced to near poverty by the combination of the War and taxation, and the Club was a welcome refuge from the gas meter in a one-room flat off the Gloucester Road. Equally, there were some exotic members possessed of great wealth, such as Nubar Gulbenkian. Nubar was the son of Calouste Gulbenkian, known as Mr Five Per Cent, which was the royalty he had negotiated on the entire production attributable to the Iraq Petroleum Company. He was an amazing sight – huge bushy eyebrows, a beard, monocle, orchid, morning dress and spats were his everyday wear. Heaven knows what he wore on special occasions! He was fond of hunting and was out one day with the Quorn sporting, as usual, an orchid in his buttonhole.

'Never seen anyone out hunting wearing an orchid,' snorted the choleric Master.

'I don't expect you have seen an Armenian Jew out hunting before either,' Nubar replied.

The most unpleasant member was Laurence Gresley. He was the brother and heir of Sir Nigel Gresley, a baronet. He occupied the same chair every day for about twenty years and issued a stream of venom about his fellow members when he was not sipping barley water, coughing or declaiming about his sex life to anyone who would listen. We doubted whether, in fact, he had any sex life at all, although there was a Yugoslavian lady with a basement flat in Eaton Square known as the Balkan Mattress – she was very popular with some of the members.

The centre of gravity was the backgammon room and each evening it was packed with mostly rich and charming idlers, amongst whom was the ill-fated Lord Lucan, of whom more anon. There were some delightful older members who played virtually every day and I recall in particular Michael Stoop, a very brave Grenadier, a Greek called Kryiakides and known as Kaos, and Nico Tollenaar, a distinguished Dutchman of great wealth but very slow movement, known as the Flying Dutchman.

There was also David Milford Haven, saturnine ex-Naval hero, and Andrew Bowring, a bad-tempered alcoholic who, when he started to lose, said 'I think *I* will keep the score in future!' and Jerry Gurney, a handsome stockbroker who decamped with his secretary to Spain and was never heard of again. He was understood to have pushed the button that fired the torpedo that sank the *Bismarck*.

Of the younger members, I became friends with Paul Irby, an old Etonian stockbroker possessed of discretion and courage (he once rode in the Grand National) who was a partner in the firm of Vickers da Costa of which Winston Churchill's brother, Jack, had also been a partner. Others included Ludovic Kennedy; Demitri Kasterine, a photographer and mentor of Patrick Lichfield; Rupert Deen, who very successfully did (and does) nothing at all; Desmond Seward, the historian; together with an assortment of other egregious characters.

Ludovic Kennedy became a close friend. A complex and charming character, he allowed himself to be scarred by what he judged to be the disgraceful treatment meted out by the Admiralty to his father, the heroic Captain of the *Rawalpindi*, a merchantman which sank after ramming a German battle cruiser. Many assumed that he was awarded the Victoria Cross whereas the reality was that he was not decorated at all owing, according to Ludo, to a blot on his escutcheon at the Admiralty following an act of folly during the General Strike in 1929, when he was put in charge of a Naval detachment tasked with managing striking Welsh miners. Ludo's entirely understandable resentment at his father's treatment led to his always being on the

Mother (1950s).   Father (1950s).

On the schooner *Heatherbell*, with two proper mariners (1950).

R: Aboard the troopship *Devonshire* – Colonel Fraser (the Razor, centre) eagerly anticipating our arrival in the jungle. James Cheetham (left) looking wistfully towards London.

L: Captains Cluff and Fazil. Guards Parachute Company, Cyprus, 1963.

Father, Turnberry (1958).

Uncle Willie in conference in Madrid (1949).

Looking
rather camp
in Moscow
with local
friend
(1969).

Garden,
Cheshire
(1958).

Nicky Phillips and Annunziata Asquith. AC doing an impression of a butcher on holiday, Grasse (1969).

Demetri with Capucine at La Colombe D'Or in Saint-Paul de Vence.

!!!

Clockwise – Nicholas Villiers, Paddy Pakenham, Dennis Walters,
Bridget Walters, AC, Andrea von Stumm and Inez Franck.

Opening of the Freda Rebecca Mine, Bindura, Ghana. AC, the Prime Minister and Charles Powell.

No comment – Ghana (1985).

— 8/0/804

中國海洋石油總公司
CHINA NATIONAL OFFSHORE OIL CORP.

23/F JING Xin Building, Beijing China
P.O. BOX : 4706
Tel（電話）: 4663696
Fax（傳真）: 4662994, 4669007
Telex（電傳）: 210861 CNOOC CN

JGC

MJA

DT

August 27, 1991

Mr. J.G. Cluff
Chinaman
Cluff Oil Plc.

Approval of Assignment, Contract Area 24/16

Refer to your letter of August 24, 1991 and the attached copy of Deed of Assignment by and between Cluff Oil Plc, Cluff Oil Hong Kong Limited and Monument Resources (Overseas) Limited, according to Article 23.2 of Petroleum Contract for Contract Area 24/16 in the Southern Part of The South Yellow Sea of China and at the request of contractor, China National Offshore Oil Corporation hereby grants its approval of the assignment by Cluff Oil Plc and Cluff Oil Hong Kong limited of 80% of their Participating Interests to Monument Resources (Overseas) Limited in Contract Area 24/16, and the assignment shall be made by two times: first time, assign 40% of their Participating Interests (28% from Cluff Oil Plc and 12% from Cluff Oil Hong kong Limited), second time, Cluff Oil Plc and Cluff Oil Hong Kong Limited assign the remaining 40% of their Participating Interests (28% from Cluff Oil Plc and 12% from Cluff Oil Hong Kong Limited) provided that not later than 31 January 1992, Monument Resources (Overseas) Limited shall commit to drill one Exploration Well. Monument Resources (Overseas) limited shall replace cluff as Operator with effect from the first assignment.

China National Offshore Oil Corporation agrees to waive its rights of first refusal for this assignment.

Wang Yan
Vice President
China National Offshore Oil Corporation

CC: Mr. M. Ashley
CC: Mr. David Tang

I'm a Chinaman … CNOOC Approval
of Assignment letter, 27 August 1991.

My portrait by Bryan Organ, commissioned
for my 40th birthday, 1980.

Beijing signature of an oil licence with Sami Nasr, Frank Steele
(talking as usual), Sir Percy Cradock (UK Ambassador), AC and
Mr Tang Ke (Ministry of Petroleum), together with officials of
the China National Offshore Oil Corporation (CNOOC).

evangelical fringe of politics and the law, whereas had he not developed such an Establishment phobia he could well have risen to the top of the Conservative, or Labour, Party instead of limping along with the Liberals. Ludo, married to the equally libertarian and lovely Moira Shearer, enjoyed the St James's Club because, away from Moira, he could enjoy his backgammon, which he always played for far more than he could afford.

Alas, the Club was badly managed and the Committee, to their shame, threw in the towel and merged with Brooks's. It is now a Chinese Language School. I shudder whenever I pass it and think of all those ghostly Club members who were my friends.

ૡ

I was still flourishing financially, not on account of any industry on my part, but because my father was still realising substantial profits from his investments in Kuala Selangor Rubber, Holyrood Plantation, Highlands and Lowlands and many others. I was now twenty-six, and both of us thought that a gentle introduction to the mysteries of the City of London would be prudent.

As it happened, some of my father's cash, which the sale of the family business had yielded, was managed by the Ionian Bank in Coleman Street, parallel with Moorgate. Father had been impressed with the bank's performance and the personal qualities of the two senior Investment Managers, Michael McAlister and Bruce Sturgess.

The Bank, which had enjoyed a Royal Charter as long ago as 1842, had suffered a near-mortal blow when Nasser confiscated its Egyptian assets at the time of Suez. Its shares, at rock-bottom price, had been acquired by two stockbrokers of contrasting character and background – Michael Behrens, flamboyant bow-tied extrovert with strong artistic interests, and Johnny Trusted, brusque, shy and alcoholic. They had formed Behrens Trusted, stockbrokers, in the 1950s, and the firm had flourished. However, controversially they elected to play a fiscal anomaly for all it was worth, thereby forcing the Treasury to close the loophole known as 'bond washing'. Simply put, this was a procedure that – incredibly – enabled tax that had never actually been paid to be clawed back.

When they donated a substantial sum for the cleaning of the fabric of St Paul's Cathedral, the wags observed that Behrens Trusted had switched from bond washing to Cathedral washing. With their unpopularity growing they decided to acquire the Bank, sell the overseas banking business to The Popular Bank of Greece (where it thrives to this day as The Ionian and Popular Bank of Greece) and manage the London business as an old-fashioned merchant bank.

This they did with skill and determination, building up a team of imaginative and creative individuals, including Sam Hamburger, John Spicer, Christopher Brett (known for some reason as Inky), Michael Gaze, Stephen Cockburn, still working in the City, and a board of non-executives which included Hugh Fraser, the aristocratic Tory MP for Stone, and Godfrey Bostock, a clever industrialist from the north-west. It was through him that my father was introduced to the investment management side of the bank, and it was to this department that I was initially attached. Bruce Sturgess and Michael McAlister were the senior managers. McAlister was a Price Waterhouse-trained accountant from a rich Anglo-Brazilian family, and had served in Paris as the Duke of Windsor's Private Secretary; he always sported a handsome pair of cufflinks that the Duke had given him. Discreet though he was, it was evident that he had little time for the Duke and a lot of time for the Duchess. Michael had a heart of gold and could not have been more a more understanding and unselfish tutor. I regret that I took full advantage of his good nature.

I had by now left the Wilton Place flat and, still incorrigibly spoiled, installed myself at the Savoy Hotel for two months before moving into a flat in Eaton Square. My father had given me a 3.4l Jaguar car for my twenty-first birthday with a personalised number plate, JC 21, and I drove this to the office, arriving at about 10 a.m. Lunch was usually a prolonged affair at the Contango Club in Throgmorton Street, a dive where the principle activity, other than alcohol, was backgammon.

છ૭

A feature of life in the City of London in those days (and indeed of other institutions) was the importance of lunch. It is quite difficult to believe now that we did indeed drink and eat (mostly drink) on the scale that we did. Lunch with our brokers, Panmure Gordon, in the 1970s would more than likely start with a couple of pink gins, a copious amount of white and red wine during lunch and a glass of Kummel and a cigar afterwards. For most of the Panmure Gordon lunching years their senior partner was Ian Cameron, the father of our Prime Minister. He shared the role with a laid-back and intelligent ex-Life Guards officer, John Lithiby.

Ian Cameron was affable and shrewd and had courageously dealt with the consequences of being affected with poliomyelitis in the 1950s. Not only did he conquer it but, despite numerous operations which had shortened his legs, he became a proficient footballer. The one thing we were all proficient at was polishing off a bottle of Kummel between us before navigating an erratic route back to our respective desks. However, notwithstanding the abbreviation of the length of the working day by the three hours reserved for lunch, business was still despatched, although by 6 p.m. the City was effectively closed, there being no bars, clubs or restaurants open after that. Nowadays there has been no diminution in the alcoholic intake – it has just been deferred until the evening. Panmure Gordon are still our stockbrokers, although I have not lunched there since 1979 – maybe they have abolished it altogether.

The City certainly had a sense of humour in those days. Lord Benson was the senior partner of Cooper Brothers, the accountancy firm, whose office had long been in Gutter Lane, just off Gresham Street. One day the Lord Mayor received a letter from the self-important Benson, which read along the following lines.

> Dear Lord Mayor, in view of the international distinction of Cooper Brothers my partner and I feel it would be appropriate to rename Gutter Lane "Cooper Lane", in honour of our firm.

He received a quick response from the Lord Mayor.

> Dear Benson, We have no objection to Cooper Brothers changing their name to Gutter Brothers, but Gutter Lane will remain Gutter Lane.

The Savoy Grill, now effectively destroyed by American owners, was in those days the City's West End outpost and numerous Rolls-Royces and Bentleys would be anchored outside from 12:30 to 3:30 p.m. whilst their owners attacked the bill of fare with gusto. My father was very friendly with Cecil Moores, the owner of Littlewood's Pools, and they would often lunch there with the Chairman of the *News of the World*, Sir William Carr, known as 'Pissing Billy'. There would be three pink gins lined up by the barman in the same small bar off the Strand (now abolished) before they lunched, always at the same tables. This persisted through much of the 1980s but is unknown today.

I should add that the City lunch was a successful British export. At the instigation of my friend Evelyn Cromer, who worked there, I remember lunching with the Chairman of a famous British trading company in Hong Kong. My mission was to persuade him to support our oil exploration objectives offshore China. I was unsure as to the best moment during lunch to raise the matter, but to my dismay he lit a large cigar and promptly fell asleep. Did etiquette require me to sit patiently until he awoke, perhaps even falling asleep in sympathy, or should I grasp him by the shoulder and shake him awake? In the event the cigar detached itself from his lifeless fingers and came to rest on the trousers of his tropical suit – with a yelp he arose like Lazarus from the semi-dead.

Evelyn had an irascible father, Rowley, who had been Governor of the Bank of England. At around this time my friend Christopher Fildes was contemplating writing a book about the post-War history of the Bank and was keen to interview the extant Governors. Only one of them failed to respond – Evelyn's father. Christopher asked me if I could persuade him to relent and I eventually managed to arrange for the three of us to lunch at the Berkeley Hotel. To my relief Rowley was very friendly and at about 4 p.m. we staggered out of the dining room covered in Kummel and cigar ash, Christopher having secured the information that he sought. Two mornings later I happened to be scanning the *Telegraph* obituary notices to find that they were led by 'the Earl of Cromer', for whom seemingly that had been the last supper!

I knew very little about anything financial, and calculating gross redemption yields was 'not my scene'. On one occasion the Bank was contemplating buying a mail order business called 'Headquarters and General', which had its office in Holborn. I was deputed as part of a team to analyse the books and our party set off in my Jaguar to do so. As I was parking my car in front of the building I observed a little boy relieving himself on the front steps. 'Maybe that boy knows something we don't know,' I said to my colleagues, but we pressed on and bought the business, only to discover that the boy had indeed selected the right target.

The Bank, however, had a string of successes, amongst which was the formation in 1966 of Oil Exploration Holdings to invest in the UK North Sea. This it did most successfully, although it was sold far too soon. It was my superficial knowledge of this investment model that whetted my appetite for the North Sea oil business.

The Bank had also managed to avoid property lending and therefore emerged unscathed from the 1974 secondary banking crisis (by which time I had long since moved on). However, the Bank of England reacted strongly to the crisis and sent their inspectors in to determine all the smaller banks' exposure.

What they found at the Ionian was a clean property book but substantial borrowing on the part of Behrens and Trusted themselves, and they were told that their overdrafts must be promptly repaid. The only method of repayment available to them was the sale of the Bank itself, which proved impossible in those disturbed times.

The Bank accordingly closed, reducing the unfortunate Trusted to insolvency. I remember finding him drunk, leaning up against a pillar, and putting him in a taxi back to his flat in Regent's Park. Behrens was more robust and retreated to his lavish country house in Henley-on-Thames.

❦

After the General Election in 1966, I tired of the Ionian Bank and decided to visit New York where my Grenadier friend, Jasper Larken, had gone to live and work, marrying a beautiful girl of aristocratic Danish ancestry, Caroline Little. Her father was the theatre critic of the *New York Times*. I have in front of me the paper knife given to me by Jasper and Caroline for my role as best man at their wedding.

Another friend from Stowe, Everts Fulton, a wholly delightful eccentric destined for an early death, also lived in New York. His stepfather was Captain Douglas Williams, long-standing Defence Correspondent of the *Daily Telegraph*, bridge player and habitué of the St James's Club.

John Lindsay, a charismatic lawyer, was Mayor of New York at the time and I obtained an introduction to him from a charming old-fashioned Wall Street figure, W. Palmer Dixon. Palmer was very kind to me, providing lunches at the Racquet & Tennis Club, an institution of which I am now a member, and which possesses the finest collection of sporting books I have seen anywhere.

I was attached to a speech-writing team, for this was the election year, and legend has it that I wrote the speech that lost the election for some junior Congressional candidate. Apart from lunching with Cardinal Spellman in his residence, and being impressed with his secular concern at the dismal performance of Wall Street, I was achieving very little and I concluded that, as my reservoir of cash was dwindling, I should return to London and apply myself to earning my living.

❦

My experience at the Ionian Bank had aroused my interest in the oil business and I had met an ex-Amoco executive in New York, who had set up a so-called independent oil company with another interesting ex-Big Oil executive, John F. Tolleson. Their company, Transworld Petroleum, operated from one room in New York, and I quickly realised that one of the rules of the oil business was that the more grandiose the name the smaller the company. I had just arrived back from New York when I read in the newspapers that the British Government was opening a large swathe of new licences in the North Sea. Destiny called.

5

THE NORTH SEA

The announcement of this round of bidding for North Sea licences was accompanied by a statement that the Government was hoping that British companies would respond vigorously to the opportunity. From my time at the Ionian Bank I realised that the chances of any British companies responding, apart from BP, Burmah (then solvent!) and Shell, were slim. I studied the small print and realised that, by reason of the so-called discretionary system of awards, no cash was required at the application phase, the Government wisely preferring to attach work commitments to the licences rather than to auction them.

The award process was vested in the hands of the Petroleum Division of the Ministry of Fuel and Power. This was handled at that time by an uncelebrated but universally respected civil servant named Angus Beckett. He correctly saw his duty as being to ensure that the

North Sea be explored as rapidly as possible and he judged that this purpose was best achieved by having a mix of licencees, ranging from major oil companies to the so-called independents or junior exploration companies. I concluded that that policy represented a once-in-a-lifetime opportunity for an entrepreneur to enter the fray.

With the help of a firm of stockbrokers, Myers & Co, I formed CCP North Sea Associates as a special purpose company. The shareholders in CCP, other than myself, were mostly friends of mine from my Army days, including Patrick Lichfield and Nicholas Villiers, together with Tony Lambton, Sunny Marlborough (the son of Bert), Hugh Reay (then husband of one of my closest friends, Tessa, a formidable and beautiful woman now married to Henry Keswick). Others included Nicholas Phillips (dead by his own hand), Anthony Wigram, a clever, strong-willed property expert, and Demetri Marchessini, a Greek shipowner also of strong and robust personality. Demetri and I dined together once a month for close on half a century, until his death this year. I find it hard to come to terms with his departure. Irascible and eccentric he was, but also a man of character and decency.

All of these individuals showed commendable foresight as well as robust confidence in myself, and it was gratifying to see that confidence well rewarded. It was thanks to Tessa Keswick, whom I had met at a dinner party hosted by Demetri Marchessini, that I met Hugh Reay and Tony Lambton (at that time Under Secretary of State for Air). I visited him at his office at the Air Ministry where he was lying prone on a sofa. An enigmatic figure with his dark glasses and languid voice, his investment of £50,000 became worth £1 million within a very short time. It is a curious feature of the English that if you lose them money they feel sorry for you, but make them money and they become suspicious and fractious. As a thank you for his gains he sent me a pair of cufflinks (which I have lost) and I increasingly heard anecdotally that he was fond of saying, 'That fellow Cluff is an absolute shit.' After his political downfall he retreated to a villa in Italy where I last saw him in about 1980. He kept on telephoning me and the conversation was always the same.

'Hello Algy, how's the North Sea?'

'The North Sea is very well, thanks Tony.'

This was repeated over and over again for three years.

Hugh Reay was quite a different character. When I first became aware of him – he was a member of the St James's Club – he affected a wing collar, an orchid and always carried a cane (a sort of poor man's Nubar Gulbenkian). With his skeletal good looks and high intelligence he was quite intimidating, but the reality was that he was the kindest and most beautifully mannered of men. His younger son, Ned Mackay, is my godson. His second wife, the clever and attractive Victoria Warrender, was a friend of mine, although our relationship cooled a little after she broke her leg falling off a five-bar gate that I had commanded her to climb.

Sunny Marlborough's investment was smaller than that of his fellow aristocrats, but nonetheless very welcome to him. Anyone who made Sunny money was immediately promoted to friend and I was included in the Blenheim Palace shooting list. Initially I was slightly out of my depth – I had the pleasure of shooting there for forty years, but was never advanced from Number One or Number Eight in the line. After Sunny's death, happily his son Jamie has continued to ask me and, as my shooting skills deteriorate, I have finally, and ironically, occasionally made it to Number Five!

Demetri Marchessini I met in the drawing room at 90 Eaton Square, then (and now) the flat of the Rawlings family. Then, in 1969, Louis Rawlings was still alive and happily his wife, Patricia Rawlings' mother, is still living there aged 102. Demetri and I hit it off and I spent many merry holidays on his vast yacht *Deineira*. Demetri was very scrupulous about his friends, but he always had a harmonious crowd, which included the puzzling Richard

Soames, Mark Birley, Tessa Keswick and not many others. We always had the most interesting cruises around the Greek islands and I remember in particular a visit to Paddy Leigh-Fermor's house on the Mani. Demetri's father had laid the groundwork for the family's shipping fortune but his mysterious uncle, always known as 'Uncle', was usually on board and we never knew whether he was crew or guest. The family shipping business, Marchessini Liners, was satirised as the perfect way to dispose of your mother-in-law – send her on a voyage from Piraeus to New York and you will never be bothered again, as they always sank in the mid-Atlantic!

Of the other investors, Nicholas Phillips tragically cut short his own life shortly after his success with CCP. Handsome, silent (almost Trappist), he made an investment in one of the earliest business parks. A liquidity crisis arose; being proud and secretive he was unable to share his anxieties with his wife and family and gassed himself in the garage of his estate in Hertfordshire. His family included four sisters, two of whom, gifted and beautiful, were the objects of desire on my part. In fact, if I can ever be said to have lost my head it was for them.

Nicholas Villiers and Patrick Lichfield I had met whilst in the 1st Battalion of the Grenadier Guards. Villiers was one of the most competent officers, but very much a human being, blessed with a gift for mimicry. He was usually the leader of the pack, with an unerring talent for trouble. He even contrived to smuggle his girlfriend into the Officers' Mess for a week without detection. He went on to become a successful banker and a distinguished bibliophile and happily he has never lost his irreverence. Lichfield, then called Anson, was a lively, warm-hearted and somewhat maddening character but with a gift for friendship and an undoubted talent for photography. He was nothing if not a snob and his endless stories always had some aristocratic bias. He skilfully divided his life into two compartments – his successful and unconventional photographic career and his conventional weekend life at Shugborough, his family's stately pile in Staffordshire where he was always a generous host. His tendency to go slightly off the rails was arrested by Annunziata Asquith, his lovely and enigmatic consort for the last ten years of his life, which sadly terminated at a shoot where his body suddenly succumbed to the various assaults, mostly of tobacco, to which it had been subject. Alas, Shugborough was disposed of shortly after his death.

Anthony Wigram was the other large CCP shareholder. Anthony is a clever and combative character, very much his own man. With his beautiful and formidable wife Sally beside him, he has discreetly been very successful.

I had a disagreement with him concerning CCP and after a period of froideur I concluded that he had been right and we revived our friendship, which I much value. Through my friend P. A. V. (Peter) Cooper, the senior partner of Myers & Co., I was introduced to a small firm, Charterhall, who agreed through its Chairman, Derek Williams, to take 30 per cent of CCP, thereby defining its name: Cluff, Charterhall and Partners.

The consortium thereafter was Transworld Petroleum (70 per cent) and CCP (30 per cent). Committed to £1 million of seismic work, of which CCP's share was £300,000, I raised this mostly in units of £50,000. That investment was to become worth close to £1 million within two years.

My task was to raise the money and to advance the argument that, notwithstanding the obscurity of Transworld Petroleum, the Britishness of CCP should be taken into account by the Ministry.

One of the interesting features of this whole process, and I set it out as a fact rather than a criticism, was that notwithstanding it was by now glaringly obvious the North Sea was going to yield vast oil reserves, not one individual left BP, Shell, Burmah or any other large company to seek funds from the City of London to found new oil exploration companies. This of course served to reduce the level of competition and suited my book very well.

In North America, where there are as many as 30,000 independent oil companies, executives leave the large US oil companies on an almost daily basis to form new companies. The irony was that the Cities of London and Edinburgh were waiting for such executives to raise capital. None did.

As a prelude to the submission of our application, I conceived the idea of inviting Angus Beckett and his wife to dinner. This occurred at a rather rackety club known as The Clermont in Berkeley Square, the inspiration of the egregious John Aspinall (Aspers), who reduced the fortunes of large numbers of the aristocracy at the chemin-de-fer tables. However, there was an excellent restaurant where the hapless aristocrats were softened up prior to doing their duty at the tables. There was also a charming garden and it was there, on a summer's evening, that myself and the Becketts dined.

All went well and Mrs Beckett, a comely and large lady, said at the end, 'Is there a nightclub near here?' As it happened the club Annabel's, founded by the great panjandrum of good taste, Mark Birley, was and is located in a basement, and so a small staircase took us down to Annabel's. I then steered Mrs Beckett around the dance floor and a good time was had by all. When I called for the bill the waiter said, 'Oh that's all right Sir, Mr Keating has paid it.'

'Mr who?' I said, not having heard of him.

'Not that awful man Keating?' Mrs Beckett exclaimed.

It turned out that Geoffrey Keating was a PR man loosely associated with BP. He had spotted our party arriving and recognised Angus Beckett, and incorrectly assumed it would score points for BP with Beckett if he had the cheek to pay my bill. Some years later Angus explained to me that whenever he got home in the evening his wife would say, 'Have you given Algy any blocks yet?' with the implicit threat that the quality of his dinner would be governed by his answer.

❧

Geoffrey Keating was quite a character and subsequently became a good friend. The son of an Irish Nationalist MP, fat, bald and ungainly, he nonetheless had charm as well as exuding an aura of trouble, not to say danger. He told me that all he could remember his father saying to him as a child was: 'Shut up and deal!'

Legend has it that whilst he was attached as a photographer with the *Daily Mirror* to the 51st Highland Division during the retreat to Dunkirk, the Divisional Commander (blessed with the inappropriate name of Fortune), held a briefing session every evening. After he had finished a particularly gloomy summary he asked 'Any questions?' at which Keating was alleged to have said, 'You are surrounded you c—t and I'm off,' promptly departing on his motorcycle for the coast and freedom. The rest of the Division was captured the following day.

He eventually became a military PR man attached to Montgomery's staff in North Africa and, no coward, was awarded the Military Cross. He was an outstanding photographer and his work should be better known. After the War he worked for BP, particularly under the chairmanship of Sir David Steel, and despite having been sacked twice conducted his correspondence on BP writing paper c/o 3 King's Yard, just opposite Claridge's, where he lived. He briefly helped Slater Walker establish themselves in Saudi Arabia and submitted a famous invoice which read, 'To entertaining Arabs – £10,000'. To everyone's surprise he married Susie, a shy girl whose costume of jeans never varied.

Once we all went to Moscow where Ed Stevens, the *Christian Science Monitor* correspondent, owned virtually the only private house in Moscow. Stevens arranged for us to dine at the British Embassy and we all put on our dinner jackets and awaited the Keatings in the hotel lobby. They appeared from the lift with Susie still wearing jeans. I said to Geoffrey that this was going to be rather embarrassing, but he shrugged and said there was nothing he could do with her. So we set off in a convoy of limousines to the Embassy, climbed the marbled steps and waited for the footman to open the door. After a couple of minutes a woman wearing jeans appeared and said, 'Oh hello, I'm Lady Smith, the Ambassador's wife. We are having a TV supper tonight, do come in!'

Keating's stratagem at Annabel's backfired and shortly afterward Chris Dohm, Tolleson and I were interviewed at the Ministry of Fuel and Power and received a warm welcome. 'May I rewrite your application for you?' Beckett asked – and I realised that we were on to something.

An unusual episode may have contributed to our eventual success. Over a dinner in the St James's Club, we hatched a strategy derived from the controversy the press had stirred up regarding the methodology of the licensing policy and, in particular, the absence of any premium or auction element. Over four hundred blocks were to be awarded on a discretionary basis, but in deference to the press criticism, the Government allowed a handful to be auctioned off as a prelude and a determination of whether an auction system could indeed work. During our dinner we decided that, on the basis of Dohm's knowledge of North Sea geology, we should make a cash bid for a block that Dohm considered would be knocked down for a much higher sum to a major oil company. Our problem was that we had no cash, but with the assistance of the Club claret we concluded that this would be a clever way of indicating that we had (believing that no civil servant would possibly imagine anyone had bid without having the cash).

We therefore bid a large sum for a particular block in the northern North Sea. The bids were in sealed envelopes and opened in the theatre at the Central Office of Information in Millbank. This was televised, and I recall that Dohm and I sat behind the great Paul Getty. The first bid for the block was way below ours and we suffered some very anxious moments before Shell bid £10 million for it, thereby vindicating our strategy and avoiding the early termination of my oil career.

It is interesting to reflect how many new companies in the UK could have been created had there been more liaison between the City of London and the Government. The City, to its credit, was anxious to provide the funds but there were precious few applicants. A partner in Cazenove, Michael Belmont, had the vision to see this and was responsible for the creation of LASMO, one of the few successful new British oil companies born in those early North Sea days. Meanwhile, dozens of small American and Canadian companies flourished – Ranger, Siebens, Hamilton and many others became rich through the North Sea. Indeed, Hamilton brought the first British North Sea oil field into production, the Argyll Field, using a revolutionary floating production technology, thereby enriching their British partners Associated Newspapers, who had had the vision to invest. Their participation in Argyll yielded them an enormous return.

The day finally arrived when a buff envelope was delivered, offering our Consortium Blocks 21/1 and 21/6. There was much celebration, which was short-lived for poor Chris Dohm, whose hobbies of drinking copious amounts of vintage port and flying small aeroplanes had fatal consequences at a small airport in Florida a few weeks later.

Our success was very gratifying, but it rapidly sank in that we were going to need to raise more capital to pay the cost of our first well on Block 21/1. My contacts in the City of London were mostly confined to the members of the Ionian Bank, which was in no mood or position to raise funds. However, one evening I was asked to a dinner party in their house in Argyll Road by Rupert Hambro and his lovely American wife, Robin. After dinner I was regaling everyone with my exciting new venture and its thirst for more capital. The next morning one of the other guests, Neil Balfour, then working for Barings Bank, called me and said that Barings had wanted to support North Sea exploration and invited me to come to meet some of the management. This I did and Peter Cooper and I met Charles Williams (whose initials are oddly CCP) and

Derek Maclennan, two of their more conservative directors. They quickly saw the point, became our advisors and, together with Myers & Co, orchestrated our first fundraising.

Charles, a Labour man, shortly afterwards left Barings and eventually led the Labour Party in the House of Lords, whilst writing successful books on cricket, Marshal Petain and De Gaulle, amongst others. His wife Jane was once one of Winston Churchill's Private Secretaries and her son by a previous marriage is the present Archbishop of Canterbury who, curiously, was the Financial Director of Enterprise Oil, one of the few other British success stories in the North Sea.

∽

These were heady days in the North Sea, as discoveries of enormous oil deposits quickly occurred. We duly raised our share of the cost of our first well and the exploration hole 21/1-1 was drilled in 1974. As a chilling example of the chronic cost of inflation, which has beset the world, I recall the total cost of the hole 21/1-1 as being £675,000, which before the recent oil price collapse would not be much more than the daily cost of an offshore rig.

In a state of great excitement, I flew backwards and forwards to the rig from Aberdeen and happened to be on the rig when we first encountered the oil column. The column was very deep (about 800m) and led to all sorts of calculations being made by third parties about the enormous wealth we had discovered. However, we were all too aware that more capital would be needed to drill the step-out or appraisal wells to confirm the dimensions of the discovery. I was given a sample of the oil in a Colman's mustard pot, which I proudly produced at dinner that evening at the shooting lodge in Angus where Henry Keswick had asked me to stay. To my dismay Patrick Lindsay, another guest, judging me to be too cocky, threw it on the fire.

Happily it was indeed a commercial discovery and, after much argument, we named it the Buchan Field (after the nearest landfall in Scotland, but in my mind it had always been a tribute to John Buchan, my favourite author as a child). By this time Transworld Petroleum had brought in new American partners led by St Joe Minerals and I enjoyed working with our new American colleagues L. Chase Ritts III of New York and Smiley Raborn of Calgary, around which he drove in the only Rolls-Royce in that chilly city.

CCP was now valued at £20 million (equivalent to about £200 million today). Charterhall, owners of 30 per cent of the share capital, whose sole asset this represented, wanted more control over their destiny. The directors of Charterhall were very pleasant colleagues and the board of CCP felt that it was entirely reasonable to put in place a scheme of arrangement, which effectively cancelled their shares in CCP and replaced them with a direct interest on the licence. This required an EGM, resulting in a furious row with certain shareholders who opposed the scheme. Nonetheless it was approved and I believe rightly so. Peter Cooper, the Chairman, died on the 16th tee playing golf at Royal St George's in Sandwich shortly afterwards, to my great distress.

The subsequent election of a Labour Government, together with the appointment of Tony Benn as the Minister of Energy, led to a thoroughly unsettled atmosphere. A state oil company, The British National Oil Corporation (BNOC), was formed and there followed an almost lunatic period as regards waste of executive time. BNOC was initially chaired by Frank Kearton, the left-leaning Chairman of Courtaulds, and the CEO was an abrasive South African, Alastair Morton.

One of their objectives was to determine the right of BNOC officials to attend the Operating Committee meetings of those licences that had commercial reserves, which included our consortium. BNOC had settled itself in Stornoway House, off St James's Street and overlooking Green Park. It had been the residence of Lord Beaverbrook, who would most definitely not have approved of the new tenants. The so-called participation negotiations were often started by the BNOC civil servants at 5 or 6 p.m., in the knowledge that they would be likely to drag on throughout the night. It was unpleasant to be sitting with our American partners negotiating with our own Government and witnessing them behave in such a maladroit and coercive manner. I recall saying at the time that the imposition of a BNOC representative on the Operating Committee was akin to prisoners of war inviting the Camp Commandant to attend their escape committee meetings.

This all became otiose when BP acquired the Transworld consortium, including Charterhall, and Tricentrol acquired CCP North Sea Associates. I had meanwhile acquired additional offshore licences in the Irish Sea and the Celtic Sea and had formed Cluff Oil, into which I had vested my CCP shares. My North Sea involvement, which had begun in the fourth round of licensing, was over until 2014 when, after an interval of forty years, Cluff Natural Resources applied for licences in the twenty-eighth round.

Derek Williams, the Chairman of Charterhall, was a shrewd accountant but not a particularly robust character, although I became very fond of him. His life suddenly deteriorated, his marriage collapsed and his only son, driving to his first semester at a university in Texas, was killed in a car crash.

Poor Derek was devastated. The memorial service was held in St Paul's, Knightsbridge. His son had been at Eton and although the college was on holiday, the church was suddenly packed with two busloads of Etonians, a most moving experience. Derek died too, shortly afterwards.

∽

CCP was undeniably a success story and it was particularly satisfying that it had resulted in significant enhancement in the fortunes of my backers. Angus Beckett had the satisfaction of seeing his handling of the licence awards result in the creation of a huge new industry for the UK. He deserves to be more recognised ... and should our new North Sea exploration result in a commercial discovery it will be named the Beckett Field.

6

CHINA

In 1980 the Communist Government of China signalled for the first time since the Cultural Revolution that it was prepared to engage commercially with the capitalist world by inviting applications for offshore oil licences in the South China Sea and the Yellow Sea. It was widely accepted in the oil world that the Pearl River and the Yellow River had created the conditions which would have led to the deposition of hydrocarbons in commercial quantities.

The Chinese, energy bereft, were understandably anxious to develop their hydrocarbons but quite simply lacked the technology to do so. When, accordingly, they invited the international oil industry to apply for licences, most companies were galvanised by the opportunity. Amongst them was Cluff Oil. Since the end (for us) of the North Sea saga, we had scored a modest success in

Australia by floating the first non-Australian oil company on the Sydney Stock Exchange, Cluff Oil (Australia), in 1979. This involved spending a fair amount of time in Sydney and Melbourne, for part of which I was joined by my then girlfriend, Nikki Howarth, beautiful, friendly and a great help on the public relations side. We appointed Ord Minnett, leading Sydney-based stockbrokers, to advise us. This was the first oil company that they had floated and I thoroughly enjoyed our association with their senior partner, tough but charming Dutchman Gilles Kryger, and his glamorous wife Sue.

Through Geoffrey Stockwell, an ex-Iraq Petroleum Chairman, I had been introduced to Sami Nasr, a petroleum geologist who had been with IPC and had retired to Australia. IPC in those days was owned by the British and French oil companies and the Chairman was traditionally appointed by BP, the largest shareholder. Stockwell, a rather crusty but kindly person, had been BP's nominee and when I decided that China and Australia should be our next targets, Geoffrey agreed to help and joined the Cluff Oil board.

Nasr, a Palestinian, was an extraordinary individual. Whilst in Iraq he had married the Irish matron who ran the IPC hospital at, I think, Kirkuk. She was very old-fashioned and thought to be an IRA sympathiser. When Sami travelled, being a Palestinian married to an Irish lady living in Australia, he triggered every kind of security alert at airports. Sami was quite elderly by this time but was a wise and experienced man, and he quickly put together a portfolio of oil and gas properties, which generated a welcome income. Ord Minnett insisted that the board of Cluff Oil (Australia) had to have a majority of local directors and Sir Robert Norman, Chairman of the Bank of New South Wales, and Ian Harper, a senior partner of our Sydney lawyers Freehills, joined us, and very civil colleagues they were.

The shares listed at 20 cents, and within two years a local company bid 80 cents. So we went out on a relatively high note.

∽

We switched our attention from Australia to China, and our team was immensely strengthened by Alan Johnson, who became the Cluff Oil exploration manager and subsequently director. The bulk of the negotiations with the China National Offshore Oil Company, CNOOC, known inevitably as Snook, was conducted by Stockwell, Johnson, Nasr and myself, although we were assisted by Frank Steele. This was a fascinating time when all felt that offshore China was to be the next North Sea-style bonanza.

At the time the Governor of Hong Kong

was Lord (Murray) MacLehose, a tall and imposing figure to whom I was introduced by Anthony Royle, then a Minister of State in the Foreign Office.

'This is Algy Cluff, Murray,' he said, 'he is about to drill for oil off the coast of China.' MacLehose looked down his nose and said, 'There is no oil off the coast of China.'

'Stupid c—t,' I thought. 'What does he know about it?'

Alas, he was absolutely right!

I conceived a plan to fund our Chinese exploration by establishing a company in Hong Kong – Cluff Oil (Hong Kong), which would be owned by some of the larger Hong Kong trading companies. Assisted by the able young Peter Norris of Baring Brothers, I managed to induce Swires, Inchape, Sir Y. K. Pao, Wheelock Marden and the mighty Hong Kong Shanghai Bank to participate. At the time Michael Sandberg was the Chairman of the Hong Kong Bank, which took a 30 per cent interest in Cluff Oil (Hong Kong). When we made our first visit to Beijing to meet the CNOOC officials I was staggered by the warmth of our welcome. The following morning I discovered the reason for this. On a blackboard in their office they displayed a schematic chart of the corporate structure of Cluff Oil (HK). This revealed that they were under the impression not that the Hong Kong Bank owned 30 per cent of Cluff Oil but that Cluff Oil owned 30 per cent of the Hong Kong Bank. I kept my counsel.

Life in Beijing in 1981 was pretty grim, with everyone, male and female, wearing the regulation Mao suit and no motor vehicles in sight. Hotels too were a problem. Iincredibly, when you compare it to the situation today, there were only two hotels judged suitable for foreign businessmen – the Beijing, so crowded that you risked sharing a room, if not a bed, with an engineer from Texaco, and the Fragrant Hills, which was allegedly designed by the legendary I.M. Pei ... and fragrant was the word. Once Sami, Alan and I, together with our finance director, Daniel Lux, were all booked in there, and when I checked in I asked for an early call at 6 a.m. The phone duly rang and a voice said: 'Get up.' I went down to breakfast and came upon a scene of total commotion – Lux had walked through a plate-glass window and fallen three feet into an ornamental pond. The only other occupants of the dining room, to my surprise, were Red Indians wearing their feathered headdresses. To this day the only Red Indians I have seen were in China – heaven knows what they were doing there.

The breakfast was rendered additionally memorable by Sami Nasr insisting on ordering a five-minute boiled egg. I did not think he had quite communicated this order coherently and was unsurprised when eventually five eggs were placed on the table in front of him.

Finally, the day came when we were advised that we had succeeded not only in securing licences but, in the case of the Yellow Sea, being nominated as the Operator. In the UK the award of licences is hardly attended by any ceremony, as they are dispatched by third class post in a buff envelope, usually to the wrong address. In China, however, I was much impressed to be bidden to a banquet in the Great Hall of the People. There were hundreds of guests, none of whom I had seen before or since, together with Sir Percy Cradock, the wise and cynical British Ambassador, Frank Steele and myself. I sat next to the appropriately named Mr Tang Ke, the Oil Minister, and there were speeches and toasts and, all in all, it was rather a bewildering affair.

We had a red flag limousine (the Chinese Rolls-Royce) placed at our disposal and stayed in great comfort in the Dai-yu-tai State Guesthouse. After the banquet, as we were walking rather dizzily down the steps to our limousine, I said to Frank Steele, 'You know, Frank, I think we have finally found a country which really appreciates foreign investors.'

'I wouldn't be too sure if I were you,' said Frank wisely.

Three weeks later we received an invoice for $50,000 for the banquet they had 'given' us!

It was at about this point that a Pullman Coach joined our train, to borrow Winston Churchill's remark on the occasion when Sir Philip Sassoon was elected to Parliament. In our case it was David Tang, now a celebrity but then a 29-year-old lawyer. I received a couple of letters from him out of the blue, advising me that he had just finished teaching English at Beijing University and wanted to work for a Western company that had business in China. There were no Western companies engaged in business in China other than the oil companies, and he had learnt from a mutual friend, Annunziata Asquith, that I would be happy to interview him, which duly occurred, I recall, at the old Bentley's Restaurant in Swallow Street. David was very enthusiastic and agreeable, so I agreed that he could join us for a probationary period.

Shortly after he joined, my formidable and excellent PA, Camilla Dobson, told me that David Tang had invited me to dinner. With some curiosity I agreed to go. The dinner was to be in a Chinese restaurant on the Brompton Road. I was expecting to be dining alone with him and was surprised, when I asked the head waiter for Mr Tang, to be taken down some stairs and shown into a private room. Around the table were seated figures of some national importance, including Lord Chancellor Michael Havers.

I sat down next to an elderly lady who

turned out to be Lady Havers. 'What is your name?' she said to me.

'Cluff,' I said.

'What did you say?'

'Cluff,' I replied again.

'Oh Cluff, you *are* fortunate to be working for David.'

I reflected ruefully that I had clearly met my match in this young man and resolved to treat him with some regard.

കന

David and I have had some epic trips together to Zimbabwe, Chile, Burma, China and Australia. On one occasion. Alistair McAlpine sent his private jet to collect us from Singapore and fly us to Broome in north-west Australia where Alistair had a house and, unusually, a zoo. Life was rather Spartan – dinner at 6.30 p.m. and no alcohol. I think Alistair had some idea that the politicians would approve the construction (by McAlpine) of an international airport, but nothing happened and the house and zoo have reverted to bush. The place reminded me of a lesson in comparative values taught me by an old Australian stockbroker, Max Bell, who had sold two million acres in north-west Australia and with the proceeds bought a single acre in the Channel Islands!

We made an unusual visit to Tasmania

when we were considering buying the Van Diemen's Land Company, a firm established by Royal Charter which owned a huge ranch on the northern shore. We stayed the night in the only hotel in the neighbouring town of Burnie. David and I were standing at the bar and I was conscious of some dancing going on in the distance. Out of the gloom there appeared a large male who asked David to dance. He declined.

ɐ

We were now preparing to drill our first well in the Yellow Sea and opened an operational office in Tsingtao, in addition to one we had in Shanghai run by the capable and formidable Eileen Carr. The well evinced no hydrocarbons, nor did the South China Sea Well in which we had a 10 per cent interest. Although that was the conclusion of the oil venture offshore China, it was not the end of my association with Hong Kong. I had many friends who lived there at that time, in particular Simon Murray, Chief Executive of Hutchison Whampoa, David Davies of Hong Kong Land, Julian Reid, a stockbroker and yachtsman to whose daughter Sarah I have the honour of being Godfather, and Henry Keswick, who was always very kind to me and occasionally allowed me to stay in the Jardine bungalow in Shek O.

Apart from the view from my house on the White Cliffs of Dover, I have found nothing to compare with sitting on the veranda at No 9 Shek O, watching the ships ply their way through the South China Sea. Much later, in 1997, Tang, Davies, Murray and I formed the Anglo-Hong Kong Trust as a demonstration of solidarity with the Hong Kong Chinese in the run-up to the reversion of sovereignty to China. As far as I was concerned, this largely focused on a campaign for a more even distribution of British passports. We had some success with the Trust, but hardly consonant with the effort we invested in it. However, it was an enjoyable period and led to the formation of the first business school in Hong Kong, primarily through the energy of David Tang and the generosity of Dickson Poon.

The Anglo-Hong Kong Trust had about twenty members, mostly from leading Hong Kong Chinese business or banking dynasties. We felt impelled to form the Trust having seen the bitterness of many Hong Kong Chinese, who felt that they had not been properly – if at all – consulted about what was after all *their* future. Our purpose did resonate in certain quarters as we were invited to dine on board the Royal Yacht when Prince Charles visited Hong Kong, and the whole of the Trust went to lunch at No 10 Downing Street with John Major who, with characteristic courtesy and good manners, showed us around the place before lunch. Sustaining a lively conversation at lunch brought Murray, Tang, Davies and me into a muck sweat as our Chinese friends resolutely resisted any encouragement to push the conversation along. In desperation I asked a rather grim man, T. T. Tsui, if he could say anything about the current Beijing policy on security in the South China Sea. He looked at me, took a toothpick out of his mouth and said, 'You come Hong Kong soon?' I sank back in my chair and looked apologetically at the Prime Minister, who to his credit seemed quite unsurprised by his inscrutable guests.

7

THE *SPECTATOR*

One day in 1980 I was lunching with Henry Keswick, who was then the proprietor of the *Spectator*, in John Aspinall's new gaming club just off Sloane Street. Aspers, as he was known, was at another table, and judging we were discussing the *Spectator*, shouted, 'Don't sell it to him, Henry, he's too left-wing.'

A few weeks later Henry rang me and asked if I did indeed want to buy it. I assured him that I did. The share price of Cluff Oil was buoyant; I was forty years old and anxious to continue touching life at as many points as I could sensibly do. Had I been more cautious I would have registered Ivan Fallon's warning in the *Daily Telegraph* the day after my fortieth birthday, which I had marked at Claridge's with a dinner dance. Fallon, citing the excesses of the party as a possible catalyst, penned a tongue-in-cheek article entitled – Is THIS THE END OF THE OIL BOOM? As it happened he was correct – it was indeed, although my birthday party played no part in it. But the die was cast and I had accepted Henry's offer. The price was £160,000 and I paid it in Cluff Oil stock. Henry had himself bought the magazine five years before from a bounderish character, Harry Creighton. Had Creighton owned it today it would be the UKIP house magazine, as Creighton was driven by a loathing for all things European.

Creighton was at one point both Editor and proprietor, and this lethal combination drove the circulation down to 11,000 copies. When he sold it to Henry he kept the paintings and prints that had adorned the office walls for many years. I sought to rectify this when I bought the magazine, and I lent the office a series of Max Beerbohm caricatures and some moderate oil paintings, one of which was of Winston Churchill wearing the full dress uniform of the Lord Warden of the Cinque Ports, painted by Bernard Hailstone, a friend of mine who did two equally terrible pictures of my parents. It was stolen.

Legend has it that Henry, being very grand, only knew one journalist, Alexander Chancellor, who had been a contemporary at Eton. Alexander was also comparatively grand, being a son of Sir Christopher Chancellor, once Chairman of Reuters. Although he was the lone candidate for the Editor's chair, it proved to be a wise choice as Alexander quickly rescued the magazine's reputation. I was rather intimidated by my new possession and not entirely confident in my role of proprietor. Part of that role, I judged, should involve the determination of policy. I could not have been more wrong. I learnt this lesson when I dispatched a memorandum to Alexander proposing that there should be more coverage of the Far East. This he printed as a letter as if it were from a reader! I realised I had met my match.

In fact, matters of policy were very soon otiose as both the magazine and I were struggling financially; Ivan Fallon's prediction of the end of the oil boom had come good, and substantially reduced my company's share price, so accordingly my scope for financing a loss-making magazine. The contributors had to be paid weekly (not a lot I concede) and every week, for a time, James Knox (Managing Director) and I had to prostrate ourselves before various unsympathetic bank managers.

James is a cultured man of steel and possessed of all the attributes that help in a constant state of crisis – humour, a sense of the ridiculous and imperturbability. He also has a first-class brain. The crisis certainly brought out the best in us and we laughed merrily as we lurched from one bank to another. Some evil man at a bank called the Marine Midland did manage to return all the contributors' cheques once, but incredibly that was the only occasion.

We eventually discovered a bank, Drummonds, with a manager, George Macdonald, who not only appreciated the point of the *Spectator* (both institutions had been formed at the end of the eighteenth century), but realised that with the right management it could become a successful business, which indeed it did. When I bought it, the magazine was losing the equivalent of about £1.5 million a year in today's money, and when I stepped down from the board twenty-five years later it was recording a profit of £1.5 million. The magazine still banks with Drummonds.

Although the Editor had revived the magazine's reputation, and had put in place a coven of contributors of the highest calibre (A. N. Wilson, Ferdy Mount, Auberon Waugh, Murray Sayle and the artist John Springs amongst them), all was clearly not right. At that time I had a friend who owned a magazine of commerce. His office was diagonally opposite the *Spectator*, which had now moved to 56 Doughty Street. Often he would call me at midday and report that I would be pleased to learn that the Editor had arrived for work but that, half an hour later, the Editor's team had adjourned for a well-earned lunch at the Duke of York's Public House. At 4 p.m. he reported that most of the team had arrived back in Doughty Street prior to setting off home for another rest. Alexander also experienced some turmoil in his private life. A further issue arose when Alexander fired A. N. Wilson as Literary Editor for altering a book review by Bel Mooney, hardly a sackable offence. Andrew Wilson was and is a good friend and his appointment as Literary Editor, in my view, sucessfully complemented his work as a novelist and biographer. I began to think I had to get a grip.

The ship began to steady itself following the appointment of Charles Moore as Deputy Editor in 1982. This was at Alexander's suggestion, although I was charged with the task of persuading him to join the magazine. He was a leader writer on the *Daily Telegraph* at the time and was understandably anxious about joining us, given the perilous financial state of the magazine. However, I must have done a reasonable job for he agreed to our offer. Part of the attraction, it subsequently became evident, was Alexander's promise that, were Alexander to leave, I should appoint Charles as his replacement. This I had forgotten when, after much indecision on my part, I decided that it was in Alexander's own interests as well as that of the Spectator that he should be asked to resign. I had developed a great affection for Alexander, which was why I dithered before finally making the decision.

In those days I frequented a bistro in

Wardour Street called Chez Victor, which bore the legend on the window 'Le Patron Mange Ici'. The Patron was a splendid character who wore a toupee, but only at weekends. I invited Alexander to lunch at Chez Victor, having finally resolved to ask him to resign. When I blurted out this information Alexander exhibited little surprise; in fact when I disclosed that I was proposing a £25,000 termination payout he positively beamed. He was aware, he told me, that I had been considering replacements for him ranging from Germaine Greer to Richard Ingrams, but gently reminded me that Charles Moore had been given to understand that in the event of Alexander leaving he, Charles, would replace him. Happily for the magazine, he duly did.

There followed for me a difficult few days with some retribution threatened by a few of the contributors, although I was greatly cheered that weekend when I rang Ferdy Mount and Bron Waugh, to be told that they had no quarrel with my decision. Simon Courtauld the Deputy Editor also resigned in solidarity with Alexander and I was persuaded to pay him £20,000, a substantial sum in those days. About fifteen years later I had cause to call the magazine and to my surprise the call was answered by a familiar voice.

'Who's that?' I enquired.

'Simon Courtauld,' was the reply.

'I thought I paid you £20,000 to leave in 1985,' I said. 'What are you doing there?'

'I am reading the magazine for libel,' Simon (a qualified barrister) replied.

'Well, can I have my £20,000 back, please?'

The line went dead.

Nonetheless, I hold Simon in high regard. It was at my instigation that he wrote two of his many books, a history of the *Spectator* and a biography of the egregious Derek Jackson.

8

Libel, and
Other Magazines

The magazine continued its slow march to prosperity as Charles built on the Chancellor foundations and the circulation doubled. In fact, to our astonishment, it became apparent that we were in danger of making a profit, the first in living memory (for which at least part of the credit was due to James Knox and his successor Louis Dominguez, a handsome Argentinian known by the hacks as 'Louis Dominguez on drums') and it became necessary to conceal this welcome fact from the contributors who were hardly well paid, believing the magazine to be impoverished.

It was during Charles' editorship that my role converted from proprietor to Chairman. In 1985 I had been approached in London by Malcolm Turnbull, a clever Australian lawyer and now Australia's Prime Minister, on behalf of Kerry Packer, to enquire whether I would consider selling the magazine. I had not thought of doing so, although I was beginning to realise that the days when it was appropriate for the *Spectator* to be owned by an individual were over. The magazine should, I thought, be part of a larger group, which whilst respecting editorial integrity could provide a secure base with management strength. So although I spurned the approach from Packer (I never liked him anyway), by a complete chance I was on a business visit to Sydney and received a note in my hotel room from Fred Brenchley, an executive Editor with the Fairfax group, asking whether I could meet him and the CEO for a drink.

Fairfax then owned the *Melbourne Age* and the *Sydney Morning Herald* and the Fairfax family had been the proprietors for over 140 years – I believe the longest continuous ownership of newspapers in the world. They told me they had finally determined to expand their business into Europe and had concluded that buying the *Spectator* would be a foot in the door from which they could observe the scene preparatory to making a much larger acquisition. I liked them all, including Sir Vincent, Sir Warwick, and James Fairfax. I never, however, met the 26-year-old son of Sir Warwick, known as Wacky.

When I flew back to London I had a cheque with me representing an option I had provided them to purchase the magazine, subject only to a cursory examination of the books and a meeting with the Editor. I had no doubt that delivering the *Spectator* into such strong hands was the correct decision. I had assumed that would also spell the end of my association, and I was surprised and delighted when James Fairfax asked me to remain as the Chairman of a newly constituted board. The previous board had included a rubber planter (Charles Letts), an Irish peer (Hugh Rathcavan), and a Tory MP (Dennis Walters). The new one, which survived for a further twenty years, included Pat Sheehy, Owen Green and John King (chairmen respectively of BAT, BTR and British Airways), alongside Norman Tebbit, Christopher Fildes, Peregrine Worsthorne, André Deutsch and Ludovic Kennedy. The meetings were generally harmonious, although a bit of sulphur was apparent between Messrs Sheehy and King, and the appointment of Tebbit (an excellent non-executive) triggered the resignation of Ludovic Kennedy, which we all judged as an act of silliness on his part. Christopher Fildes played a key role, being a *Spectator* contributor with a sound knowledge of the publishing business, unlike the rest of us. He is wise, kind and thoughtful and once delivered himself of my favourite business aphorism. 'The thing to remember about emerging markets,' he wrote, 'is that you cannot emerge from them!'

The meetings, held at 6.45 p.m. in my office, were always attended by the Editor and the publisher and included the Editor's report and a commercial discussion (the increasing cost of paper clips, as Ferdy Mount thought) before we adjourned to Brooks's Club for what were always convivial dinners for congenial guests.

Coincidently with my ceding ownership to Fairfax there occurred the crisis at the *Telegraph* group. Aware of this, Fairfax advised me that they would value an introduction to Nicholas Berry, the son of *Telegraph* Chairman Michael Hartwell, as they were keen to acquire a 25 per cent shareholding and to refinance the *Telegraph*. I arranged a dinner between Nicky and various Fairfax executives. Sadly, following representations from two of the *Telegraph* non-executive directors to Rothschilds (who had been appointed by the Berry family, not by the *Telegraph*), panic ensued and an unknown Canadian, Conrad Black, seized the moment and made one of the most brilliant opportunistic moves in Fleet Street's history, without Rothschilds apparently conducting any due diligence into him whatsoever. Black borrowed £15 million, which was all that was required to refinance the newspaper, and a year later it was to record a profit of £50 million.

The final event of note that marked my tenure as proprietor was a libel case, which was as unusual as it was unnecessary. It cost me a great deal of money and should never have come to court, and would not have done were it not for the casual nature of the *Spectator*'s libel lawyer, Richard Sykes, who scarcely deigned to discuss it with me before, to my horror, we found ourselves in front of Mr Justice Otton in the Strand. The plaintiff was an Argentinian socialite who had at one time been married to the motorist Henry Ford (as well as three or four others). At the time of the alleged libel the incumbent husband was a Mr Marcie-Rivière. The origin of the libel was an article that our High Life correspondent, the legendary Taki Theodorocopulos, had written concerning a ball which Mrs M-R had given in Los Angeles. According to Taki, the ball had largely been attended by gay men dressed as women, owing to the hostess's shortage of female friends. This carried the byline 'D Gay Day'. Unknown to us at the *Spectator*, Taki had sent this to Mrs M-R, accompanied by a letter on his own Cadogan Square writing paper warning her that this article was to be the first of many. (I never discovered the cause of his dislike for Mrs M-R but by the end of the trial I had come to endorse it!)

By this time it was August and, like many rich people, both Taki and, unknown to him, Mrs M-R had taken off to the Greek islands, Taki enjoying the hospitality of a Mr and Mrs Goulandris on their private island. One day

Taki's hosts were invited, along with their house party, to lunch on Mrs M-R's neighbouring island. As the Goulandris launch came alongside the jetty, Mrs M-R, in Taki's account, caught sight of her nemesis. She screamed, 'I will not have *that* man on my island!'

Mrs Goulandris, being a decent lady, ordered that the boat be turned around, and she bore the house party back to her island. This was deadline day at the *Spectator*, and Taki was always scrupulous about filing his copy (although the magazine was not always so scrupulous about reading it for libel). The source of our subsequent problems was Taki's next column, of which the first line – hardly Shakespearian – read: 'I have today been humiliated by a geriatric Circe with a face like a collapsed cake.'

That insult proved the last straw for Mrs M-R, and very soon we were all sitting in court in front of Justice Otton. I had not been consulted about the selection of our QC (a geriatric Etonian) or about the process known as 'paying money into court' (which caps the level of libel damages). The plaintiff's solicitors were Carter-Ruck and their QC was an intelligent, owlish individual called Hartley (whose father had masterminded PLUTO to deliver fuel after the Normandy Landings). Carter-Ruck had an array of multi-coloured files in front of him whereas Sykes' filing system seemed to be contained within a Sainsbury's shopping bag.

Unusually, half of the jurors were women, all of whom sported faces that looked to me like collapsed cakes. So we were off to a bad start. It quickly became apparent that we were doomed.

Our problems were compounded when Taki, as exasperated as I was with Sykes' uselessness, took a swing at him in front of the jurors as we all moved to adjourn for one of the innumerable breaks which seemed to characterise a day in the courts.

By this time I was no longer proprietor, but had remained Chairman thanks to James Fairfax. We were finished and I had to foot the colossal bill, to which Taki with his customary generosity made a contribution. Nearly all the combatants other than Otton, Taki and myself are now dead.

එ

When Sir Warwick Fairfax died, his son, also Warwick, a 26-year-old born-again Christian recluse, was persuaded by some Australian bankers to borrow $2.7 billion to buy the rest of his family out of the business, the plan being to repay the loan by floating the *Melbourne Age* and the *Sydney Morning Herald* off on the Stock Exchange. Alas for this strategy a Wall Street crisis arose, Warwick went bankrupt and the *Spectator* came up for sale again. Conrad Black, now proprietor of the *Telegraph*, bought it. Once again I thought my *Spectator* association was over; however, Andrew Knight, at the time Conrad Black's Chief Executive, asked over lunch at Brooks's if I would like to stay on as Chairman. I am grateful to both Conrad and Andrew for this, as I carried on as Chairman for a further fifteen years. During that period I had the pleasure of working with four more Editors, for by then Charles had been correctly promoted to Editor of the *Sunday Telegraph*.

He was succeeded by Dominic Lawson. I have a high regard for Dominic. As a friend he is always the best company and as an Editor he was highly professional, taking immense trouble with the contributors' copy and securing scoops that served to sustain the magazine's renaissance.

Whilst Dominic was Editor he rang me up one day and said he was going to remarry. After congratulating him he surprised me by asking me to be his best man – surprised in the sense that I am twenty years older than him. 'Of course I would be honoured,' I replied, 'but don't you have any friends?'

'No,' he said firmly.

Dominic also moved up the hierarchy at the *Telegraph* to replace Charles at the *Sunday Telegraph* when Charles was appointed to edit the *Daily*. The next *Spectator* Editor, Frank

Johnson, was not so agreeable. Curiously self-destructive, he set about systematically upsetting all those with whom he needed to work closely – namely Dan Colson, the easy-going Chief Executive; Kimberley Fortier, the publisher; and myself. At the first board meeting he attended he made a great display of looking at his watch, sending out the signal that he had another appointment. I accordingly pushed the meeting along, and afterwards Pat Sheehy, Norman Tebbit and I adjourned to have dinner at Wiltons. At the next table, dining on his own, was Johnson – probably charging it to the *Spectator*! He was shortly succeeded by a much more congenial colleague, Boris Johnson. It is no insult to him to relate that he was blessed with a Managing Editor, Stuart Reid, self-effacing and competent, who really got the magazine out every week.

Part of the agreeable charade of our board meetings involved a presentation by the Editor. Whilst Boris was the Editor the board meetings were always attended by Conrad Black and Barbara Amiel, by then his wife. I had known her before the marriage and she had been quite a friend. However, she treated me with polar indifference after she became Lady Black. It was to Boris' credit that he was not remotely fazed by the presence of the proprietor and his wife, his preparation for the meetings manifestly having been conducted in his head on his bicycle on his way to the meeting.

A Deputy Editor of the *Spectator* at this time was Simon Heffer, a fine journalist and polymath as well as being a most agreeable colleague. Had I still been the proprietor when Dominic Lawson was appointed Editor of the *Sunday Telegraph* I would have advanced Simon to be Editor of the *Spectator*.

෯

It was now that Conrad Black's empire began to crumble. The catalyst was his dismissive treatment of questions from an American fund manager, Tweedy Brown, at the Hollinger AGM. Soon Conrad was abandoned by his influential friends as the authorities began examining alleged corporate governance abuses and in particular certain so-called non-compete payments, which he ill-advisedly awarded himself. He was arrested, tried and imprisoned. I wrote a lengthy letter to the Court in Chicago on his behalf, citing the benign aspects of his proprietorship. However, it was all over; he began a six-year prison sentence and Lazards was appointed to find a buyer for the *Telegraph* and hence for the *Spectator*. Boris and I worked hard to put together a management buyout should the new purchaser not wish to retain the *Spectator*. Alas the successful bidder, the Barclay Brothers, wished to do so. Within days of their bid prevailing I was summoned to their offices in St James's Street and beneath a portrait of Charles Clore by Graham Sutherland was advised that they wanted no independent directors in their business. I would have done exactly the same had I been in their shoes, but nonetheless it was rather a sad day after twenty-five years as proprietor and Chairman.

⁓

For various periods in the 1970s and 80s I had also owned four magazines – *Apollo* (twice!), the *Literary Review*, *Quarto* and *The Vole*. *Apollo* I had acquired in partnership with my friend Naim Attallah, a Palestinian of intelligence and charm who first came to prominence in London as the Finance Director of Asprey and who is credited with reorienting its business away from selling ivory hair-brushes to the English landed gentry to very expensive baubles to the Arab world. John Asprey implemented that strategy with consummate skill, turning a moribund business into a highly successful combine.

Our opportunity to buy *Apollo*, then a wholly owned subsidiary of the *Financial Times*, came about during a torrid episode for the *FT*, mostly due to the industrial strife that had engulfed all of Fleet Street. The arts magazine, although respected, always limped along in the shadow of the *Burlington* and *Apollo's* tyrannical Editor, Denys Sutton, would not respond to any proprietorial suggestion. Naim attempted to exercise commercial control whilst my sole function was to endeavour to exercise any sort of editorial control over Denys. This function I fulfilled by lunching and dining him at various five-star restaurants where I hoped to enlist alcohol as my ally in penetrating Denys's severe mask. In the event we became firm friends without, however, my securing the faintest degree of influence over him. Naim and I finally resolved to terminate his role and gave him a grand send-off at a dinner at the Royal Academy.

We persuaded Anna Somers-Cocks to leave the Courtauld and replace him and she required all of her considerable intelligence, beauty and charm to cope with the irascible Sutton during the handover. Shortly afterwards, Naim and I were approached by a rich German, Mr Flick, who bought us out. Subsequently Flick tired of it, sold it on to a Swiss collector and, some years later, I persuaded Conrad and Dan Colson to buy it for one pound and it now sits as a *Spectator* subsidiary. I asked Michael Hall, Deputy Editor of *Country Life*, to edit it, which he did with style and common sense, accepting our advice that to compete with the *Burlington* was futile. He redirected the magazine to a new constituency of rich and private collectors, a formula that I believe has worked well enough.

Naim's and my next collaboration was the acquisition of the *Literary Review*. I think it came about as a suggestion from our friend Auberon Waugh, who eventually became the Editor. I admired and respected Bron, whom I had come to know through the *Spectator*, where for a period he was, inter alia, the wine correspondent. Reviewing a red burgundy he described it as tasting '… like dead chrysanthemums on the grave of a stillborn West Indian child.'

After a short period, I handed my shares to Naim who gamely soldiered on for some years before selling it to Christopher Ondaatje. I arranged the transaction although Christopher proved rather too mettlesome for Naim's taste.

9

ZIMBABWE

One day in 1980 I was lunching with Geoffrey Tucker, an agreeable cigar-chomping political public relations consultant whose waistline testified to the Herculean culinary challenges he set himself every meal, breakfast included. He had asked me to meet Tony Barber, previously Chancellor of the Exchequer and then the Chairman of the Standard Bank. Barber, a decent and modest man, had just returned from Zimbabwe/Rhodesia where he had attended the independence ceremony. He explained how surprised and impressed he had been with the country and argued that if Ian Smith had achieved nothing else by his wilful declaration of Rhodesian UDI, he had at least prevented the kind of socialist ideological orgy which had ruined the economies of all those African countries that had secured independence in the 1960s. He explained

that the white population was in a catatonic
state following the victory of Prime Minister
Robert Mugabe's army, but that the opportunities, particularly in the mining industry,
were there for the taking as the country had
been effectively abandoned by that industry. I
was rather bruised by our Chinese experience
and the mining industry had more appeal to a
company starved of exploration funds, for the
obvious reason that minerals are there to be
discovered at much shallower depths than is
the case with hydrocarbons, and therefore the
company's exploration dollars go that much
further.

What Anthony Barber said made sense and
a couple of days later I set off for Zimbabwe
and set up my base in a suite on the top floor
of the Meikles Hotel in Harare. I quickly
grasped that 'catatonic' was certainly the
condition of most of the white farmers and
businessmen whom I met, friendly and
generous though they were. I met Robert
Mugabe and a number of his Cabinet minis-
ters, including Bernard Chidzero the Finance
Minister, Richard Hove the Defence Minister
and the Governor of the Reserve Bank (something of an oxymoron since there were no
reserves), Kombo Moyana. To present the case
for Mugabe in today's world is challenging.
However, I must record that in many respects
he was an interesting individual. UDI had
been a foolish and unnecessary act by Ian

Smith's government. His foolishness was no
better exemplified than by his statement that
UDI was the commencement of a thousand
more years of white rule. In fact, eleven years
later they had been defeated in battle. Mugabe
had been arrested and interned by the Smith
regime and during this confinement his only
child by his first, Ghanaian, wife fell sick and
died. He was not permitted to visit the dying
child in hospital nor was he allowed to attend
the funeral. In such circumstances it shows
admirable fortitude on the part of Mugabe
not to have executed Smith, let alone to spare
him a trial. Instead, he allowed Smith to sit
out his retirement in his Harare house, from
where he never issued a repentant or generous
word.

Similarly, Mugabe's relationship with the
white farming community, whom he orig-
inally protected, was not reciprocated. The
fact that five thousand white farmers owned
75 per cent of the best land in the country
was clearly an impossible status quo to main-
tain. Mugabe used to tell me that when he
toured the country the black population's
constant refrain was, 'Where is the land that
we fought for?' Mugabe responded that they
should be patient, as the farmers were earning
the foreign exchange which the country badly
needed. But the white farmers did not have
the wisdom or judgement to meet him halfway. Had they offered to voluntarily surrender

part of the land, not to mention embarking on programmes to train young African farmers, the land situation may not have spiralled out of control in the unfortunate way it did. The British Government bears a measure of culpability here too. At the Lancaster House Conference in 1980 a sum of £40 million was promised to the Zimbabwean Government, which could have been utilised to buy out some of the farmers on a willing buyer/willing seller basis. For some undisclosed reason the money was never delivered, prompting Mugabe to argue that he had been double-crossed by the British. In the dying days of John Major's Government some effort was made to resuscitate that situation, only for it to be repudiated again by Blair's government under pressure from the Secretary of State for International Development, Clare Short, who idiotically argued that taxpayers' money should not be applied to buying out Colonial white settlers. So the inevitable happened.

In May 1994 Mugabe came to visit us in Scotland, where we had lined up some potential African investors, and so we organised a piper from the Gordon Highlanders to be present on his arrival. The piper gradually built up steam and, observing the spectacle, Mugabe turned to my wife Blondel – 'Unless I am mistaken, this gentleman has an ostrich feather on his head? Under his arm he is squeezing the gut of a dead animal? And he is wearing a skirt? And they call *us* primitive!'

಄

I was forty years old at the time of my first visit to Zimbabwe and virtually all my commercial life during the following thirty years was committed to Africa. From that suite on the top floor of the Meikles (I think I was practically the only guest) I put it about that we were looking for a local exploration manager. I selected Nick Graham, chain-smoking and highly strung, but an intelligent and creative geologist who had previously worked for Falconbridge, a large Canadian mining company. My brief to him was quite simply to get us a cash-flow as rapidly as possible and, within nine months, the Royal Family Mine near Bulawayo was on production. It was, I believe, the first open-cast mine in Africa to utilise the Heap leach cyanide process. Shortly afterwards we moved up a few gears and launched the Freda Rebecca Mine at Bindura about sixty miles north of Harare. This was the country's largest gold producer.

The Freda Rebecca Mine was to produce 100,000 ounces of gold per annum. It was called Freda after my mother (who exhibited no interest in responding to this compliment by visiting the eponymous operation) and Rebecca after Nicholas Graham's daughter.

119

It was Graham's job to bring the mine onto production, ably backed up by a strong Dutchman, Max Kraan, and it was my responsibility, inter alia, to raise the capital. This process involved me in prolonged negotiations with Dr Moyana, the then Governor of the Reserve Bank. Moyana told me that at his weekly meeting with Mugabe the first question from Mugabe was invariably, 'How many white men have you killed today, Governor?'

After a week of meetings with him I was reading a book in my room at the Meikles Hotel on a Saturday evening when I experienced a lesson in African clarity and probity. There was a knock at the door at about 6 p.m. I opened it and there was no less than the Governor in a tracksuit. Help, I thought, he has come to propose a brown envelope arrangement. He said, 'May we resume our negotiations?'

'Of course,' I replied.

'But first may I use your bathroom,' said the Governor.

Being English and therefore used to euphemism I assumed this meant he wished to respond to the call of nature. 'Please go ahead, the bathroom is over there.' After an hour and a half he emerged ... having had a bath.

We finally obtained the $20 million necessary to advance the mine to production and were casting around for a celebrity figure to open it. As it happened the British Prime Minister, Margaret Thatcher, was due to visit Zimbabwe and I suggested that she might endorse UK PLC by opening the mine in the presence of Prime Minister Mugabe. This was duly agreed and tremendous preparation, ensued for the visit. I had known the Prime Minister in my North Sea days and had been invited to dine at Downing Street on one unhappy occasion, during which a collection of us oil producers was castigated by her for complaining too much about the tax burden.

She was flown by helicopter to a landing zone about a mile from the mine. The route was lined by African schoolchildren, none of whom had the faintest idea who she was, and were instructed to chant 'Thatcher, Thatcher' as the cavalcade rolled past. Unfortunately the Jaguar car we had with difficulty procured for her came to a juddering halt halfway and she had to be transferred to one of our Land Rovers.

After the ceremony and the speeches, we adjourned to a marquee where there was much speculation as to whether Denis Thatcher would be able to access a gin and tonic. This was provided and just as the marquee fell silent, Denis was heard saying, 'Absolutely useless these chaps, I assume!'

~

Harare had its own stock exchange and we resolved to list our subsidiary's shares in order to raise some local capital. We also saw this as an opportunity to set up a trust for the mineworkers and vested 10 per cent of the shares in the trust. I believe this was the first occasion, in what was then termed Black Africa, that a company had done so and it served admirably to align the interests of the workers with that of the management. Under Max Kraan's firm but fair style of leadership we never lost one day to industrial action. It was at about this time that we appointed Godfrey Gomwe, a black Zimbabwean, as Finance Director and he eventually succeeded Roy Pitchford, an engaging white Zimbabwean, as the first African Chief Executive of a mining company in Africa.

We also employed a young English geologist, Andrew Woollett. I judged that he had flair and common sense and I despatched him to do a report on what other African countries we should engage with. Our financial position had improved, as had our reputation, although Zimbabwe continued to be viewed unfavourably by the stock market. I asked Woollett to look at a number of countries, the criterion being geology – our imperative – not politics. The two countries we selected as targets, Ghana in West Africa and Tanzania in East Africa, both yielded excellent results, although ironically our success eventually proved to be our nemesis.

☙

Around this time the board was considerably strengthened by the appointment firstly of Sir Thomas Pilkington and then of Sir Patrick Sheehy. Tommy Pilkington and I have been friends for many years now and, if anything, our friendship served to strengthen the corporate governance of the company because of the regard in which I hold him. Tommy is the sort of discreet patrician who has lived a hard-working life as a landowner, member of the racing fraternity (at one point Chief Steward of the Jockey Club) and for many years Chairman of T & J Harrison, a Liverpool-based family shipping company primarily engaged on Caribbean and African dry cargo work. He is shrewd and sensible and we have shared a number of adventures together in Africa, particularly to Zimbabwe, Tanzania and Zanzibar. Some of my happier days have been spent shooting at his estate in Hertfordshire, where he has always lived with his wife Susan and which is now run by his son Richard.

Pat Sheehy is a robust, powerful and highly intelligent retired Chairman of BAT industries where, after national service in the Irish Guards, he spent his professional career. He is a thoroughly intimidating individual, physically and mentally bearing resemblance to a caricature of capitalism. The reality is that he is the kindest of men and one of the exemplars of the best of UK industry in the twentieth century. I was very fortunate to have had the support and advice of Tommy and Pat during those Africa years.

We were also joined by Zimbabwean geologist Douglas Chikohora, who had previously worked for RTZ. Douglas and I have visited innumerable African countries since then and he remains in partnership with me, scrutinising African opportunities.

&

I had first visited West Africa as a soldier in the British Cameroons in 1961 and those vivid experiences of a vanishing Negro civilisation (and environment) affected me strongly. There was the visual impact engendered by jungle, by the mysterious Cross River, by the fabric and patterns of the female attire and their smiling tactile welcome. My next visit to West Africa, after twenty years, was to Ghana with Douglas Chikohora. We had a couple of days in Accra meeting the Ministry of Mines officials, which included a country visit to Obuassi, the site of the main operating hub of Ashanti Goldfields. We were shown around by Sam Jonah, whom I was to meet again when we were taken over by Ashanti in 1996.

Ashanti at the time was controlled by the controversial Lonrho company, whose charismatic CEO 'Tiny' Rowland had skilfully put together a hotchpotch of assets throughout Africa, including car dealerships, newspapers, farms and mines. He had an arresting effect on small shareholders but was anathema to professional investors.

Ashanti was an old Colonial gold mining company still blessed at this time with significant high-grade reserves. After the Second World War Major General Sir Edward Spears had chaired the company. He was undeniably able, but somewhat out of step with the times. He wrote well on military history, but it is not clear why he was selected to chair Ashanti, knowing nothing of business or mining. An example of his autocratic, not to say eccentric, management style was afforded by his annual visit to Ghana to chair the company's AGM at Obuassi. His arrival (with his secretary) was preceded by the despatch of the company's Rolls-Royce, which was shipped over from Southampton to Takoradi for the sole purpose of conveying Sir Edward from Takoradi to Obuassi and back again. It was not surprising that the clever Rowland spotted a vulnerable takeover opportunity in Ashanti, and to his credit he acted.

Rowland was an interesting if rather sinister

figure and achieved virtually heroic status amongst his shareholders. He was of German/ Indian origin and was alleged by his numerous enemies to have served in the Hitler Youth. His parents settled in the UK and were interred on the Isle of Man during the War, during which one of them died, fuelling Tiny's dislike of the so-called 'Establishment'. He was believed to have made his fortune during the Berlin Airlift in the late 1940s and then, after a skirmish with the Inland Revenue, emigrated to Southern Rhodesia.

He was a tall, handsome man of commanding presence and it was during those early Rhodesian days that he metamorphosed into a local character, gifted as he was with humour and intelligence. He put together a number of farming and mining properties and his break came when Angus Ogilvy, the aristocratic husband of Princess Alexandra, was despatched to Salisbury (Harare) by his Chairman Harley Drayton. Drayton was a leading City figure, and he wanted to see what could be done to advance the future of London and Rhodesia Lands, a moribund but quoted company. The local Standard Bank manager gave a lunch for Ogilvy to which he invited Rowland. Rowland, exuding maximum charm, cast his spell and ensnared Ogilvy in his web. As a consequence, Rowland exchanged his local assets for shares in what was then renamed Lonrho. As a further consequence, Ogilvy's future was doomed as he became too closely associated with Rowland's buccaneering activities, eventually having to retreat from all his commercial appointments to spare the Royal Family embarrassment.

Rowland, cleverly realising that Africa was on the cusp as a result of the doom of Apartheid, forged close relationships with the first generation of African leaders, flying them hither and thither in Lonrho's private jet and applying his ruthless charm to great effect. He was aided by Ogilvy and Alan Ball, his Deputy Chairman, together with a gaggle of non-executives whom he famously dismissed as 'lights on a Christmas tree'. As the market capitalisation of Lonrho grew, the balance sheet became more and more stressed by the quixotic conduct of the African countries and the difficulties of sustaining cash remittances to support the dividend policy. Having exhausted the use of Ogilvy, Rowland turned to two ex-Conservative politicians for support – Duncan Sandys and Edward du Cann. But by this time the City had had enough and clamoured for the application of what is now called corporate governance.

An enquiry into the affairs of Lonrho was launched, primarily at the instigation of Edward Heath. This report is an astonishing document and deserves to be reprinted if not filmed. Rowland, with his extraordinary recall, ran rings round the inspectors and so the enquiry, which had really been initiated to remove Rowland and Ball, failed entirely and the 'straight eight' (as the reforming non-executives were known) were all removed, leaving Rowland and Ball in command. Along with his contemporary Jimmy Goldsmith, Rowland can be congratulated for bringing capitalism to life. Saturnine and sinister he may have been, but he built up a conglomerate that benefitted many thousands of African workers (none of whom he met). The company effectively died with him.

ॐ

Within a short time, we had identified and developed the Ayanfuri Mine in Ghana and I forged a friendship with President Jerry Rawlings and his glamorous wife, Nana. As President he formally opened Ayanfuri, flying himself in by helicopter. He breakfasted on rashers of bacon and a bottle of whisky and marched out in front of the three-hundred-strong audience of workers and local tribesmen. It was the only time I have ever heard a politician tell his audience what they did not want to hear. He delivered a wholly admirable tirade against idleness, selfishness and so on, which was not rapturously received. As Francis Johnstone, one of our executives, remarked, 'I would have followed him into the jungle after that.'

Ayanfuri was funded by a loan from Barclays and by Albert Abela, a distinguished Lebanese businessman of great charm and integrity. He had built up one of the world's leading industrial catering businesses, primarily feeding the oil companies in the Middle East. I had met him through Dennis Walters, a long-serving Tory MP with Arab connections, who was a non-executive director of the *Spectator* and came up with the idea of selling advertising debentures. Albert subscribed more out of the kindness of his heart than any other motive and we became very close friends, a friendship which happily and unusually has descended a generation as his son Albertino, as kind as his father, is a very close friend of my family.

Ayanfuri proved to be a successful enterprise for all of us and so, emboldened, we looked further afield. Peter Cowley, a geologist, quickly realised the potential for gold on the shores of Lake Tanzania. Peter had been persuaded to join Cluff Resources by the Technical Director, Dr Michael Martineau, an intelligent alumnus of BP Minerals, and Peter and I have worked together on and off ever since. Peter was convinced that the Lake Victoria area still contained large quantities of recoverable gold deposits, despite having been worked before the last war. In competition with the major mining companies, including Anglo American, we set out to prove to the Tanzanian authorities that Cluff

Resources was the right company for the project. We had a number of meetings in Dar-es-Salaam with the Ministry of Mines. Peter Cowley persuaded a delightful ex-Minister of Posts and Telegraphs, Freddie Machauru, to function as a country manager and many were the meetings we held in the rooftop restaurant of the dilapidated hotel Kilimanjaro on the coast of Dar. In London we held an important dinner for the Minister of Mines (later the President), Colonel Kikwete. This, in view of his military background, we held at the Cavalry and Guards Club in a private room known as the Bridle Room. It was here that I set out my strategy, which was that in the event of our making a commercial discovery of gold we would return 20 per cent of it to the Government. The Government could then use that as the basis for a state mining company. It is my belief that that this offer determined us as the successful bidder.

In any event we were awarded the licence to what is known as the Geita area on the shores of Lake Victoria. Our exploration rapidly confirmed the wisdom of Peter Cowley's exploration philosophy and we were congratulating ourselves on the prospects of a glittering future when I received an invitation to dine with Sam Jonah, the Chief Executive of Ashanti Goldfields. Our party was about to be ruthlessly extinguished. I had scarcely speared a piece of smoked salmon before

Sam took an envelope out of his pocket and handed it to me. This, it transpired, was a proposal on behalf of Ashanti to 'farm in' or take a stake in the Geita licence by covering all the exploration costs. I expostulated that we were not ready to reduce our stake in the project as we needed to determine its size first. He then took another envelope out of his pocket, which was a bid for the whole company! The Cluff share price was 45p, and the bid was 104p cash, or higher in Ashanti Goldfields paper. Li Ka-Shing's Hutchison Whampoa owned 29 per cent of Cluff and had committed their stock to Ashanti, thereby rendering our task of rejecting the Ashanti offer virtually impossible. In any event our non-executives concluded that the premium offered over our share price was too attractive to shareholders. Although they paid too much for our Zimbabwe and Ghanaian production they secured the real prize for nothing and terminated the existence of a company that would certainly have evolved into a multibillion-dollar enterprise. Such is capitalism!

10

AFRICA

Our board, advised by Samuel Montagu, formally accepted the Ashanti offer, which went unconditional in March. There followed a sad period for me personally as I watched the business that I had built up – and more particularly the workers in Zimbabwe, Ghana and Tanzania – come under different control. Sam Jonah and Mark Keatley, the Finance Director, behaved courteously, but a different culture now prevailed.

My final contribution was informed by an element of comedy as Sam asked me to arrange for him to meet Mr Mugabe. This I did, and so we all gathered at State House one March evening. Mugabe marched into the room radiating hostility and brandishing the offer document (recommended by my board). Sam opened the proceedings by thanking Mr Mugabe for allowing us to make this courtesy visit. '*Discourtesy* visit!' Mugabe shot back, and then treated us to a declamation on the evils of capitalism in general and of the mining industry in particular. Sam and I endeavoured to explain the fiduciary duties of public companies and then got into a muddle as I argued that the 29 per cent that Hutchison Whampoa owned of us represented effective control, while Sam found himself arguing that the 29 per cent that Lonmin owned of Ashanti did *not*. Mugabe then rounded on me and accused me of being concerned solely with profit rather than Africa and the workers. By this time I was becoming pretty angry myself, as I reflected ruefully that I was virtually the only businessman who had shown any confidence in him or his country and that this was a fine way to thank me.

Mugabe suddenly terminated the meeting and gestured to me to go into an anteroom, where there stood a man covered in hand grenades and machine guns. As the three of us were standing there I decided to regain the initiative. 'When I reflect on what I have done for you and your country,' I said, 'I am amazed that you have could have the effrontery to speak as you just have.' Without waiting for him to reply or for the hand grenades to go off I walked out, only to remember that I had sent my car away and had to walk the two miles back to Harare, every step accompanied by an uncomfortable feeling in the small of my back that a shot was about to ring out.

That was the final chapter in the history of Cluff Resources. Geita became the Geita Mine with reserves of 20 million ounces. Ashanti subsequently became casualties of an ill-conceived hedging arrangement and were able to stave off disaster by selling half of Geita to Anglo American. Geita is now one of Africa's largest and most profitable gold mines and contributed to a major upturn in the economy of Tanzania. The Geita Mine is now featured on the Tanzania bank notes.

❦

I was fifty-six years old and still ready for another challenge in Africa, whose geological charms were at last beckoning many of the larger organisations. I was pleasantly surprised to be invited to a lunch at Anglo American's head office in Johannesburg attended by a number of their senior executives, including Bill Boustred, Kevin Williams and Tim Wadeson. This led to lunch with the Chief Executive, the remarkable Julian Ogilvie Thompson. Julian is a striking figure well over six foot tall, with a shock of white hair and a rather intimidating, although not unfriendly, manner. Not only does Julian have a first-class brain but he also has a capacity for retaining information that I have seen equalled only by Conrad Black, a very different character.

One evening there I took my wife to the

Rand Club for dinner in the Ladies' Annexe. She may have been the first black lady to have dined there, for the waiters (in white suits) burst spontaneously into applause. A touching moment.

I believe Anglo had been impressed by the way we had built up a business in Africa and in particular by our securing the Geita licence in Tanzania. They offered to finance a new company, Cluff Mining, and appointed to the board three of their senior executives, Peter Gush, then Deputy Chairman, Bobby Danchin, then head of new business, and David Fish. Both Peter and David alas died quite soon thereafter, the latter in a car crash en route from Johannesburg to Knysna. Peter Gush contracted a mystery disease, which was never explained, but caused him to gradually lose control of his voice and limbs. It took him two years to die and it was profoundly depressing to observe his distress. Bobby Danchin happily remained on our board for many years.

Cluff Mining initially focused on the Congo – or the Democratic Republic of the Congo, a misnomer if ever there was one. Doing business there, I became fond of saying, was akin to being in love with a beautiful woman who was not in love with you. At the time Anglo retained as a consultant geologist Fred Cornwall, a most sympathetic and civilised individual who had spent most of his Anglo career in Northern Rhodesia (Zambia). He alerted my attention to the existence of what he maintained was the largest undeveloped gold deposit in the world, Twangiza in the Eastern Congo. I was intrigued by this and discovered that Twangiza, together with other gold and tin deposits, was owned by a Belgian company known as Sominki. I resolved to pursue this company and was ably assisted by yet another ex-Anglo executive, Belgian economist Luc Smets. With the help of a firm of Belgian stockbrokers we tracked down the Sominki shareholders and gradually accumulated a controlling shareholding. Much time was spent in Brussels where Luc and I had a grand and interesting time planning our strategy. In this we were assisted by the then Prime Minister of the DRC, Kengo Wa Dondo, a highly intelligent half-Polish academic.

In order to impress Kengo I arranged a grand dinner at Spencer House in his honour and contrived to persuade De Beers to share the cost. My wife escorted Mrs Kengo on a West End shopping trip and that evening as we sat down to dinner I congratulated myself on a job well done. However, after we had finished the first course a gentleman in a grey suit materialised, holding a piece of paper which he showed to the Prime Minister. It appeared that during the first course he had been removed as Prime Minister in a sudden coup in Kinshasa. The rest of the dinner was an anti-climax to say the least.

We also made a number of visits to Kinshasa when it became apparent that we had competition in the form of a junior Canadian mining company, Banro, and its Chief Executive Arny Kondrat. We did not see eye to eye but eventually a compromise was reached, which involved Cluff Mining being appointed the operating company and exchanging our Sominki shares for Banro stock. Had we sold their stock we would have served our shareholders very well. However, we suddenly received a writ from Banro suing us for non-performance as operators. This was a travesty as our intention was to ensure that we fulfilled all our operating duties responsibly, whereas Banro was solely concerned about advancing their share price. Instead of ceding the ownership we elected wrongly to fight and we all wasted a lot of time and money before it was resolved. We disposed of our Banro shareholding and I vowed never to revisit the DRC, however compelling the geological argument. Luc Smets, a dogged and valiant colleague, is now retired. He presides over a large family that includes his son-in-law Matt, Britain's leading cartoonist, and Martin Newlands, one-time Editor of the *Daily Telegraph*.

Subsequently Cluff Mining became predominantly a platinum company in South

Africa and the acquisition of various licences on the Bushveldt Complex near Pretoria brought with it uncongenial colleagues with whom I was thoroughly unhappy. I considered, with the support of my board, ejecting one of them but my wife, wiser as ever than her husband, suggested I liberate myself, return to the gold business and again regain control of my destiny.

So I formed yet another eponymous company, Cluff Gold, prompting someone to suggest that the next one should be called Cluff Off! Cluff Gold operated a medium-sized open-cast mine in Burkina Faso, the Kalsaka Mine, which produced about 60,000 ounces per year. Burkina Faso at this time was enjoying a period of stability and I relished my visits to the country and to the mine. The company also owned two gold deposits – Baomahun – in Sierra Leone and another in Côte d'Ivoire. The Baomahun deposit belonged to Ronald Winston, a long-standing friend of mine from New York. His father, Harry, the founder of the famous firm of diamond dealers and retailers Harry Winston Inc, had been advised that this area of Sierra Leone was highly prospective by an American professor. Ronald, himself a metallurgist, is commercial, kind and boasts great experience of Africa, having had numerous adventures in Angola, in particular whilst buying diamonds from Savimbi. I negotiated with Ronald, mostly in his New York office on Fifth Avenue and we finally agreed an exchange of Cluff Gold stock for Baomahun. I regret that our technical team did not fully understand the deposit and it remains undeveloped. The other deposit, in the Ivory Coast, had been acquired by Douglas Chikohora and me from BRGM, the French Government mining company. That is now a significant operation.

ভ

During the Icelandic volcanic eruption in 2010, which practically paralysed the world for two weeks, I happened to be in Burkina Faso – the one place not to be since there were only two flights per week out to Europe in normal circumstances. I had gone there for a three-day visit but it was ten days before I could exit via Ghana and Dubai to Paris. Not only did I run out of books to read but also the various pills which are essential in the lives of the over-seventies. I had plenty of time to think. I had been brooding for some time over the chronic cost of inflation in the mining business, which was compounded by the lacklustre performance of the gold price. I always considered that gold, notwithstanding its obvious merits, has many enemies. Amongst them unfortunately are the bureaucrats who control the international Reserve Banks. To them a high gold price suggests that they are not conducting their affairs properly and they have the power to limit rises in the bullion price. A long-standing friend of mind, Norman Lamont, once taught me a lesson when I enquired of him how frequently the subject of gold had featured in the Treasury's deliberations whilst he had been Chancellor of the Exchequer. He could not recall any occasion. This served to put the gold price into perspective for me. Surrounded by people who are obsessed by gold I realised that we in the business exist inside a rather unhealthy bubble. Sitting in my bedroom at the Kalsaka Mine deprived of books, pills and cigars I brooded on this and resolved that the time had come for another change. So I decided to return to the North Sea where I had begun my commercial life.

I therefore resigned from Cluff Gold and began assessing the wisdom of returning to the North Sea after an absence of thirty-five years. I formed yet another vehicle, Cluff Natural Resources, and listed it as a cash shell on the AIM with the intention of purchasing some North Sea oil or gas production. In the event we concluded that the prices demanded were excessive and happily we elected not to buy any production. We then built up a portfolio of licences, which we judged to be suitable for the conversion of coal into gas. This concept we believe will be of great strategic importance when we have to buy all our gas elsewhere. We also applied for North Sea gas licences in the twenty-eighth round in 2014 and were pleased to be awarded eleven blocks. We are now engaged in acquiring reserves of oil and gas in the North Sea. Full circle!

11

Friends of the Past

Professor R. V. Jones

One evening at Christmas in 1985, I was watching a programme of lectures on measurement given at the Royal Institute in Albermarle Street by the Professor of Natural Philosophy at the University of Aberdeen, R. V. Jones. I was so enchanted by the gentle but compelling control which the Professor exercised over his audience of children that I wrote him a fan letter and there evolved a close friendship which obtained until his death in 1997. Reg Jones, the son of a Sergeant-Major in the Grenadier Guards, came to play a significant role in Britain's history but was the most modest and self-effacing of men. During the Second World War he was the Deputy Director of Scientific Intelligence. It was R. V. Jones to whom much credit is due for the application of the so-called 'window' system of air defence, which involved dropping tin foil in the path of enemy aircraft, thereby disabling their radar. It was also R. V. Jones's grasp of the importance of aerial photography that led to our identifying the rocket stations based in Belgium and to the disabling of the V1 and V2 rockets which had caused so much alarm.

At the end of the War he found himself at odds with the Labour Government and retreated into the academic world. Although he authored an excellent book of quasi-memoirs, *Most Secret War*, he was never one to blow his own trumpet and I am glad that Nicholas Berry and I persuaded our friend Winston Churchill, the PM's grandson, to secure Reg's appointment as a Companion of Honour – overdue but entirely appropriate.

Much given to pranks (which I am not), in 1941 he incorrectly diagnosed a summons to Downing Street to explain some scientific problem to the Prime Minister as a practical joke – which it was not! He was an unpompous and loveable man, and I much valued his friendship. Apart from his scientific distinction he fathered two daughters of outstanding beauty, one of whom, Rosemary, I remember well.

Paul Willert
When I moved into my first office in Park Place in 1969, as I laid the ground for life in the North Sea, I met an amiable chartered accountant called Mark Cory Wright. He was

stepping down as a partner from the firm of Dixon Wilson to pursue an entrepreneurial future by teaming up with a well-known architect, Robertson (Happy) Ward, to develop an upscale residential property complex called El Madronal, in southern Spain. We agreed to share the cost of the first-floor offices and the salary of an egregious character, D. Lux, who had been his clerk at Dixon Wilson and was possessed of a first-class brain. It was not long before I renamed Mark Cory Wright 'Maximum Capacity Wasted', as he seemed to focus on all the peripheral issues at the cost of the real issues, selling houses. He used to tell me that it was essential for the 'right' people to buy the properties. The only 'right' people, I asserted, are the ones who can afford them. El Madronal slipped out of his hands and I was left with the whole office and Mr D. Lux.

I gradually became aware that there was another tenant in the building, who mendaciously described themselves as 'Continental Development'. In fact, the office was occupied by two disparate characters – Arnold Breeme, a stocky Ulsterman, and Paul Willert, an urbane old Etonian. Both were in their fifties, but what they were doing I could not figure out. I eventually discovered that Breeme was an arms salesman, his clients being Northern Irish Protestants and arcane forces in the Yemen. There was something unsympathetic about him, whereas Paul could not have been more delightful and we became friends. I never discovered what he was really up to in the office, although he was loosely connected with Elf, the state-controlled French oil company, through their disarmingly named British subsidiary Elf UK.

Paul was the son of Sir Arthur Willert, a diplomat, and had married Brenda, a sister of the then Lord Cowdray. Before the War he had worked for the publishers Longman in Berlin and it was obvious that he was for long engaged in intelligence work, at that point assisting the Communist Party in anti-Nazi activity. On the outbreak of war he joined RAF Bomber Command and as a Group Captain he was appointed to the important role of Air Attaché at the British Embassy in Paris when Duff Cooper was the legendary Ambassador. Still involved in intelligence, he was transferred to Rolls-Royce as a Paris-based executive charged with selling engines to the French air force.

Paul had an engaging sense of humour and was excellent company. He had an apartment in Paris and a small house in Halsey Street in Chelsea. He had the judgement and the opportunity in Paris towards the end of the War to acquire paintings, particularly large canvasses by Picasso. So many did he have that they had to rotate on the walls of his small residences. I recall sitting in the drawing room of the Halsey Street house talking across the room to Paul when a mouse ambled across the parquet floor and jumped into his briefcase. 'Cripes!' I said. 'Did you see that?'

'Yes, that's Eric,' was his imperturbable and mysterious reply.

By this time Paul had shed his first wife and married Anne, the daughter of Sir Owen O'Malley, another diplomat. Always sporting his Eton Ramblers tie and usually a carnation in his buttonhole, he was an excellent companion and we spent hours and pounds lunching at Bentley's Oyster Bar or The Travellers Club. Two glasses of champagne, a bottle of burgundy and brandy, Kummel and cigars were the handmaidens of our 'frugal' culinary excursions. Not much work was conducted after them. Paul was also a member of the Garrick and Beefsteak Clubs where we also made merry. He had only one, harmless, flaw – a tendency for mythomania. Walking down a street I might observe what an interesting building we were passing. 'Oh, I was born there,' he would say.

As I wondered what Harold Macmillan's next move as Prime Minister would be, he would say 'As a matter of fact I had lunch with him yesterday.' This turned out to be a half-truth … in the sense that Macmillan had been lunching in the same building.

Paul had excellent contacts throughout the French political establishment and he arranged for Cluff Oil to develop commercial joint ventures in France, Guatemala and West Africa with Elf, leading to many more liquid lunches in Paris. Elf contained many delightful individuals but had a ruthless corporate identity and I soon learnt the lesson not to become a junior partner in a consortium managed by a large company.

Our Guatemala concession was next to an oil licence which was controlled by the estimable Jimmy Goldsmith. No shrinking violet, he raced around proclaiming that Guatemala was to Mexico what Kuwait was to Saudi Arabia, and huge fortunes were to be made. His evangelising reached a crescendo when the field was due to commence production. A great celebration was planned and the day finally came when the President of Guatemala, alongside Jimmy, stood ready to open the gold faucet that would release millions of barrels of oil. The national anthem was played, there was a roll of drums and the President stepped forward and turned the faucet. There was a gurgling noise and a huge black spider emerged ... unaccompanied by any oil.

Frank Steele
Soon after Paul retired another ex-intelligence operator, Frank Steele, joined us. He began life as a Colonial Office cadet in East Africa and became a District Commissioner in Uganda before transferring to the Foreign

Above: Frugal snack, Scotland, Laura Lindsay, Amabel
Lindsay, AC, Henry Keswick, Harry Pakenham, Patrick
Lindsay and Michael Parkin (1985).

Right: Christening of
Charlie Cluff with his
brothers, Harry and
Philip, and decapitated
godparents – Nicholas
Soames, Bobby Power
and Annunziata
Asquith.

A forest of
bottles (all
in front
of me!) –
dinner at the
Windmill.
Nicholas
Berry, Harry
(aged four)
and Blondel
(1997).

Blondel – dinner on the verandah.

Right: Hong Kong (1984).

Below: President Mugabe in the garden of David Tang's house at Sei Kung, Hong Kong. David's legendary chauffeur Alex in the background.

Rupert Deen, Furzey Island, Poole Harbour 1980, with sculpture by Sydney Harpley (subsequently stolen).

Nicholas Berry

Tessa Keswick, Greece (1982).

Sime Darby, an exemplary
animal who bit everyone
except me. Named after
a plantation company in
Malaysia.

Me at the back – do owners
resemble their pets?

Max Kraan, Blondel, Fred Cornwall, AC, Peter Cowley.
Celebrating the 100,000 ounce per annum production at the
Freda Rebecca gold mine.

David Davies, Simon Murray, David Tang and myself, Hong Kong (1990).

President Jerry Rawlings of Ghana with his wife Nana, Scotland.

Brian Alexander,
AC, Andrew
Parker-Bowles,
Nick Villiers,
Patrick Lichfield.

AC and Patrick
Lichfield at
Gunnerside.

The library at
the Windmill.

Above: Ensigns' dinner with HM the Queen, November 2013. AC third from the right, front row.

Mr and Mrs C.

Blondel, sailing in the Caribbean on Ronald and Rita McAulay's yacht *The Mamamouchi*.

No one's listening!

Office where he became a soi-disant Arabic specialist, an oxymoron in my experience. We had then obtained oil exploration licences in Dubai and Oman and thought it may be useful to enlist someone who had actually been there, although in fact he spent most of his time with us either in China or Australia.

Frank had a powerful urge in favour of horizontal rather than vertical travel and accordingly if he could go anywhere by train he would. I once called Alan Johnson in Beijing from London to advise him that Frank was on his way, to which he replied, 'From King's Cross or Waterloo?' Frank had some difficulty moving with the times and long after the invention of the fax machine was still sending FO-style messages along the lines of WILL MEET YOU AT GARE DU NORD – REPEAT GARE DU NORD – UNDER THE CLOCK – REPEAT THE CLOCK. Whenever we did go to Oman, Frank was in his element and rushed off to the Farm, the house of (Sir) Erik Bennett, an enigmatic and very clever Air Marshal who at one time commanded the Oman Air Force.

Frank and I were in Oman for the signature of an offshore oil licence and he had suggested that it might be wise for me to make a modest gift to the Sultan – *after* the award, rather than before. Accordingly, I purchased a very rare watercolour by Samuel Daniell of Muscat Harbour from Christie's. At the ceremony in Salalah I duly handed over the picture, the

Sultan nodded and gave it to Shanfari, the Minister for Oil. The next day Frank and I were walking along a street to our hotel when we passed a large Mercedes, on the rear seat of which lay our picture, on which the merciless sun had been directed for four hours, reducing its value by at least half. Being a gregarious fellow I proposed Frank for membership of the Beefsteak Club. 'Where's Frank?' someone would enquire in the office. 'In the Beefsteak!' was the inevitable answer.

Paddy Pakenham

Of my contemporaries, the most loveable and the most amazing was Paddy Pakenham, the second son of Frank, Earl of Longford, and his beautiful wife Elizabeth. Paddy would have made a brilliant Earl himself, but alas the laws of primogeniture denied him not only the title but also any money, of which, owing to his various gambling tendencies, he was constantly in need. To his father's credit, when Paddy's creditors became particularly pressing he would write a book called *God* or *Harold Wilson* or *Me* ... and the money appeared to fund Paddy's next brief attempt at cornering the coffee market. Frank Longford also wrote a book called *Humility* – 'My best book,' he apparently said.

Paddy was educated at Ampleforth and Oxford and served very briefly (about two months) in the Irish Guards before beginning a lively career at the Bar. Paddy's instability was tragically compounded by a freak boating accident, which resulted in his two closest friends being drowned – David Winn and Sara D'Avigdor-Goldsmid. They were sailing on Paddy's boat off Weymouth when the boat overturned. They clung to the hull hoping for rescue – none came and the two friends succumbed. Only then did Paddy swim to the shore, exhausted but alive.

Paddy managed to overcome this tragedy but increasingly relied on alcohol for assistance. Stories of Paddy's career at the Bar are legion. On one occasion he was defending in a drugs case. The judge was an irascible character who fancied himself an expert on drug issues. Paddy did not like him. Exhibit 'A' was the drug, which was in a cellophane wrapper. 'Give it to me!' the Judge rasped and the substance was handed up to him. He unwrapped it and took a small bite to test the evidence.

'Yes,' he said. 'This is clearly cannabis. Where was the substance found, Mr Pakenham?'

'In the prisoner's anus,' Paddy replied mendaciously.

At one point, Paddy contrived to join the chambers of an eminent and very grand QC, Lord X. Paddy's sojourn there terminated as a result of a wager for £200, won from his fellow juniors by Paddy as a consequence of the following dialogue, which ensued after Paddy knocked on his lordship's door:

'Come in – what do you want Pakenham, I am very busy?'

'I feel for you the love that dare not speak its name!'

Paddy collected £200, but had to find another set of chambers.

It was customary in court for the judges, if impressed by a barrister's conduct of a case, to send a note down to that effect. Paddy was appearing against a friend and made a forceful and eloquent closing speech. He was not surprised, accordingly, when he was handed a note by the clerk. He opened to read the simple message: 'Shambles!' Paddy discerned quickly that it was his friend's handwriting, not that of the judge.

Paddy's capacity for mischief featured in a case at Winchester Assizes. He was being led by a sententious QC, Fox-Andrews. Before the proceedings began, Fox-Andrews said to Paddy, 'Pakenham, my brokers Cazenove advise me that a new issue whose share will be listed today at 20 shillings is likely to open at a premium of 5 shillings. I have invested a lot of money in this stock and after the market opens I wish you to leave the Court and telephone the brokers and enquire what the price is.'

Fox-Andrews was on his feet and nodded to Paddy, who disappeared, had a large vodka and tonic and, returning to the Court, tugged Fox-Andrews' gown. 'Excuse me, sir.'

'Yes, Pakenham?'

'15 shillings,' said Paddy mendaciously, for they had indeed opened at 25 shillings.

Fox-Andrews gulped but bravely continued his address. An hour later he commanded Paddy to make another call. Paddy again disappeared, had another large vodka, reappeared, and said 'Ten shillings.' Fox-Andrews's face paled.

'My Lord, may I seek an adjournment for a few minutes on a personal matter?' It is not known what Paddy's fate was when Fox-Andrews discovered the real position.

Paddy would clash from time to time with a certain Judge Maude, who had married into the aristocracy and cut a rather unworldly figure. On one occasion Maude had before him two men charged with indecent conduct under Westminster Bridge. 'Oh dear,' he said, 'most unfortunate behaviour – and under such a lovely bridge too!' Another time he had to deal with a persistent drunkard: 'I think you will find a small glass of dry sherry before luncheon will be a great help.'

I was aware of the rapid deterioration of Paddy's legal career, since he spent virtually every weekend either at Nicholas Berry's house in Oxfordshire, mine on the White Cliffs of Dover or with Richard and Vivienne King in Hampshire. One Sunday evening I returned from Kent to my flat in Eaton Square to find Paddy in a wig and gown smoking a cigar. 'What on earth are you doing, Paddy!'

'I am defending a murder case tomorrow and have to get an early night,' he replied.

I could tell all was not well from his slurred speech, so I said 'Paddy, I have to go out to dinner but why don't you have a bath and take a sleeping pill and tomorrow you will be fine.' He ran a bath, took a sleeping pill; I went out to dinner and returned to find Paddy still wearing wig and gown and not much else, locked out of my flat with policemen making up the party. It turned out that he had fallen asleep while the bath was running, and for three hours water had been pouring into the flat of the 'Baron de Clara' below mine, virtually destroying it. As usual, all we and the policemen could do was laugh.

It was no surprise, therefore, to learn that shortly after this Paddy made what would be his final court appearance. He rose to make his closing speech for the defence: 'Members of the Jury, it is my duty to explain to you the facts of the case, the learned Judge will then advise you about the law and you will then reach your considered verdict.' At this point he paused, hiccoughed and went on: 'Unfortunately I have had so much to drink at lunch that I have entirely forgotten the facts, the Judge is half-witted...' But at this point Paddy's legal career ended as he was removed from the Court. This may have been a strategic masterstroke, as his client benefitted from a retrial.

Paddy died as a result, I suppose, of an accumulation of excesses – particularly of food and drink. He often, if in funds, lunched on his own with two starters and bucketful of wine – what he used to call a 'gastro-wank'. His interest in the opposite sex was also on a large scale and attended with some success. His wife Mary – to whom he was married twice – bore him three fine sons, all of whom are now married. I shall always be grateful to Richard King, also at one time a barrister, for introducing me to Paddy. Richard used to call him the 'Vicomte de Trop', an endearing and appropriate sobriquet.

Peter Quennell
I was introduced to Peter Quennell by my friend Hugh O'Neill in a bar in Fleet Street in the 1970s. Until he died, we were firm, if incongruous, friends. I was one of the four selected to deliver an encomium at his memorial service in St James's, Piccadilly.

Peter often stayed with me at the Windmill where we had marathon lunches on the veranda served by Doreen ('The worst cook in Kent'). Doreen was certainly not a good cook but she was reliable and I easily compensated for her tendency to put the chicken in the oven on Monday for Friday's dinner by buying the best local lobsters and outstanding claret. (Nicholas Phillips, then working in Lazards, Paris discovered a sale of 1961 claret, most of which we bought.)

In 1974 John Lucan, my acquaintance from the St James's Club, murdered his nanny in error (he had intended to murder his wife) and I heard the shocking news in a safari camp by Lake Rudolph in Kenya. When I returned to Kent shortly afterwards I was surprised when the doorbell rang one windy March evening. A delegation of three men in mackintoshes stood outside – this it transpired was the Lucan Squad from Gerald Road Police Station, Belgravia, and they got it into their heads that my clifftop house was exactly where the errant peer was to be found. They searched the house and the grounds without result, although I had a nasty moment when, on one of the three reinforced concrete ammunition bunkers in the grounds, they found a new door with a Chubb lock. I could not account for it. In the event, as it was a time of frequent coal strikes, the gardener, John, had during my absence in Kenya installed a back-up generator there as a precaution. That bunker is still known as the Lucan Room, and it is now my wine cellar.

The next morning the *Daily Express* sported a headline along the lines of: TYCOON'S CLIFFTOP HOUSE SEARCHED FOR MISSING EARL. Thereafter, whenever anyone with a moustache spent the weekend, a busybody would dial 999 and I would receive a visit from the Dover Police.

❦

The Lucan Room is one of the World War II reinforced concrete bunkers constructed to store heavy artillery ammunition, and which became the control room for the Wrens once stationed in the house. Here the ladies would track U-boat activity in the Channel. Ironically the Windmill had caught the eye of Hermann Goering, who had instructed that it not be bombed as he wished to remove it to his estate in Bavaria, once Britain had been conquered. Unbeknown to him a dozen Wrens were busily working to destroy German shipping from their hideaway under the cherry orchard. My wife and I have entertained two of these marvellous ladies at the house over the years (one of them the artist Lavery's daughter) and could clearly see why an armed guard was posted at the gate of the house, such was their obvious beauty.

Peter and I often dined far too well at L'Etoile or the White Tower, the latter alas long since gone. It was also where I lunched many times with the miners' leader, Joe Gormley, a very fine man, when we sought to put a North Sea consortium together between Cluff Oil and the National Union of Miners.

Quennell's wife at the time, Marilyn, was a difficult woman, although I continued to exist on good terms with her and their charming son Alexander, who nearly joined the Grenadier Guards, Peter's preference, but actually joined the film industry to which, to be frank, he was more suited.

Peter was becoming frailer in his late 70s and Marilyn banished him to a basement flat opposite their house in Primrose Hill, where my wife would often visit him. There, on introducing Peter to my wife, he spoke what she tells me she would like to be her epitaph. He held her hand, stroked it, looked her in the eye and uttered the single word – 'Fascinating'. From that moment on they were devoted to each other.

His eightieth birthday prompted me to give him a party at our club, White's, to which I invited twenty of his friends. It was not a success. I am a bit hazy about who they were, but they included Kingsley Amis. I had assumed that all these distinguished literary gentlemen would spring to their feet and deliver witty and reflective speeches so I failed to prepare anything myself. The evening ground on and more and more of White's best claret was consumed. Not a word of praise for Peter was offered. I finally gave up and brought the proceedings to a close. I walked Peter to the top of the stairs – he made it halfway then suddenly his knees buckled and he rolled all the way down to the bottom. 'Heavens, I've killed him,' I said to Charles Johnstone, the kindly poet/diplomat. Peter stood up, shook himself and took off into the night, apparently none the worse for the experience.

I happily helped Peter with financial advances against some of his work. I recall his pleasure when I told him that before going to Singapore on a business trip I bought a very expensive camera in Bond Street and a copy of *Customs and Characters*, his new publication. Engaging the hall porter in Singapore in conversation about some mundane matter I placed the £2,000 camera and the book on the table. When I turned around a discerning thief had stolen the book and not the camera!

Brian Wyldbore-Smith
In 1972 I received a curiously worded roneoed letter from the so-called Conservative Board of Finance based at 32 Smith Square. We directors of Cluff Oil had resolved in our wisdom to donate £5,000 to the Conservative Party, quite a large sum in those days. This letter was the Party's 'Thank You'. 'Dear Sir or Madam,' it began. 'I write to thank you for your gift' – here someone had written in longhand '*of* £5,000' – 'which will be a great assistance in our struggle against the evil of socialism.' This epistle was signed B. Wyldebore-Smith, Major General. Now it so happened that I knew this Major General, for

he had been the Chief of Staff in Singapore when I was stationed at Nee Soon Barracks with the Guards Parachute Company. When not in the office he was playing polo, at which my brother officer Patrick Beresford excelled, and accordingly we were all welcome guests at the Wyldebore-Smith household. So I rang him up and asked if I could offer some advice as to how to thank donors to the Party. This resulted in Brian giving me lunch at Buck's Club (of which he was Chairman).

I gently explained that to thank a donor with a roneoed letter starting 'Dear Sir or Madam' was highly unlikely to arouse any response other than indignation. Such was Brian's charm that by the end of lunch he had turned the tables on me, extracted another cheque and persuaded me to join the other Generals, Brigadiers and Colonels who made up the Party's fundraising team under the amiable and decidedly unmilitary overall command of Alistair McAlpine, a contemporary of mine from Stowe.

As we were leaving Buck's I noticed an oil painting of Winston Churchill in the uniform of Lord Warden of the Cinque Ports, which had been stolen from the *Spectator*'s office, to which I had lent it. 'Brian, that picture is mine,' I said.

'Nonsense,' he replied, 'and anyway you have far too many pictures.'

It still hangs in Buck's and that episode characterises Brian's ruthless charm.

The only mission I actually carried out with Brian was a three-day trip to Hong Kong and Singapore. This was a great success and the General and I returned with about £700,000. The only difficulty I had in Hong Kong was with a Chinese shipowner who agreed to contribute, provided I secured a place at an English preparatory school for his illegitimate child. In Singapore the tycoons were a tougher proposition. We had been advised by Alistair that the Prime Minister would consent to lunch with a donor of £250,000 or more. We met with a formidable and rather uncouth figure who owned various hotels. He offered £100,000 and enquired when he could have lunch with the Prime Minister. 'You don't get lunch for £100,000,' retorted Brian. 'Tea more like!'

I became exceedingly fond of Brian and his wife Molly – both of them wise, kind and competent and I was honoured to give his memorial address in St Paul's crypt with Lady Thatcher, a great admirer of Brian's, in the congregation.

During the following twenty years, either I or the company made occasional donations to the Party with diminishing enthusiasm, until a farcical event during Cameron's Premiership brought home the futility of it all.

Andrew Mitchell had been the shadow Minister of Overseas Development and asked me fairly regularly if we could provide some support for his private office on the grounds that it was working to foster Anglo-African relations. We accordingly donated £10,000. Shortly afterwards the Coalition was elected and Mitchell became the Secretary of State for International Development. At that time I was Chairman of a geothermal energy company, which had been approached by the then Premier of Montserrat to consider drilling there. We were amazed to learn that DFID had plans to fund the costs of these high-risk exploration wells, notwithstanding the fact that the private sector was more than willing to do so. I conveyed this argument in a letter to Mitchell. This produced a response from a lady called Beverley to the effect that in view of my financial relationship with the Minister she was replacing him as my contact. In other words, by donating £10,000 I had disqualified myself from contacting the Minister. A lesson worth learning and unlikely to render the task of fundraising the 'walk in the park' it was in the General's day.

Perhaps I should anyway have been on my guard as a result of a distinctly odd experience in the 1970s with Jeremy Thorpe. My colleagues and I, wrongly anticipating a Conservative–Liberal Coalition, had decided to donate £5,000 to the Liberal Party in addition to our support for the Tories. I wrote advising Thorpe of this and was promptly asked to lunch at the House of Commons, after which we adjourned to his office. He then explained that for various reasons he himself was in overall charge of the Party's finances and would I therefore make our cheque out to him personally. In those days I walked everywhere with my briefcase which I opened and, feigning dismay, explained that I had stupidly left my cheque-book in my office.

❧

The politician who has been the most help to me is Nicholas Soames, who has a very kind heart contained within that magnificent physique. I also cherish happy memories of his parents, and in particular Christopher, who performed a miraculous diplomatic feat in Rhodesia. I have a letter from Nicholas' late father-in-law Sir John Smith, the distinguished founder of the Landmark Trust, thanking me for saving his life, which is an exaggeration though I did manage to protect him from being assaulted by an unpleasant individual with whom he had remonstrated for cycling in St James's Park.

Lady Thatcher
Mrs Thatcher and I got off to a rather difficult start when we crossed swords in No. 10 during

her first Premiership. I was invited along with a barrel of oil executives to dinner. I was sitting on her left and we were moaning about the level of North Sea taxation and I had just said something feeble to the effect that we oil companies were just not getting enough out of the North Sea to justify the risks when she rounded on me and shot out – 'You dare to say that *you* are not getting enough out of the North Sea, *I* am not getting enough out of the North Sea.' And that was the end of the evening, at least as far as I was concerned.

I subsequently met her on many occasions and I was grateful to her for opening one of our gold mines in Zimbabwe. One New Year's Eve, shortly after Denis had died, Julian Seymour, her homme d'affaires and a close friend of mine, asked if I could give her dinner in London as she was alone. I was delighted to do so, of course, and she joined my wife, my mother (then aged ninety) and me. During the rather difficult course of the evening she addressed not one word to the ladies!

Some years later, when she was really quite frail, Julian Seymour used to have her to stay at his house at Sandwich. On one occasion I was asked across for lunch. All the guests were sat next to her for a few minutes before lunch. Assuming that she was semi-gaga I started an idiotic conversation along the lines of '… the sun is yellow, the sky is blue,' to which she responded witheringly: 'My problem, Algy, is deafness not dementia!'

Uncle Willie

My father had two brothers, of whom the younger was killed at Gallipoli. The eldest, Uncle Willie, had an uneasy relationship with my father but a very close one with me. He was a complete enigma. At the age of nineteen he had emigrated to Canada, joined the Canadian Army and served throughout the First World War. He always said deprecatingly that he contrived to avoid any fighting by running the Officers' Mess so efficiently. After the War he lived in New York where he set up a branch of the family business. My father and Uncle Willie intelligently anticipated the end of prohibition and were ready with gallons of whiskey to satisfy the pent-up demand in 1930.

Then suddenly he left New York and materialised in a suite in Geneva where he lived for twenty years, spending the weekends at another hotel alongside the lake. He had three interests – Luba, his Yugoslavian girlfriend, gin rummy (at which he excelled and played all day with his only friend in Geneva, Jim Goggin) and the ukulele. I have an excruciating long-playing record of Uncle Willie's greatest hits (privately recorded!).

When he died I was his executor and only

remaining friend. I flew out to arrange for the funeral, to be met by the saturnine lawyer who said that he had opened the safety deposit box to find it empty! I then had the melancholy prospect of going through his belongings in the suite in which he had lived for twenty years. To my astonishment he had no belongings at all, other than some investments which he generously left to me and Luba. It was as if he was one step ahead of the sheriff and the sheets were practically knotted to facilitate a rapid departure.

There followed his funeral in a Protestant church in Geneva, attended by Luba, myself and the chambermaid from the Hotel Richemond. To my shame I recall my grief during the pathetic ceremony turning to anxiety about securing a taxi as the heavens opened during the service. Willie had advised the lawyer that he wished to be buried in my garden on the White Cliffs, which rather caught me out, so I placed his ashes in the Geneva railway station left-luggage office for a week whilst I determined whether this was possible! I was very fond of Uncle Willie, but never really knew him.

12

Envoi

Success in business and the advancing years bring with them increasing charitable and voluntary responsibilities. My charitable donations included the sponsorship of *The Italian Girl in Algiers* at the Royal Opera House. I cannot recall what possessed me to do this, my music favourites being more on the 'La Mer' or 'Smoke Gets In Your Eye' level. As I recall I was given six free tickets and the use of the Royal Box for the week-long production. I have nothing against *The Italian Girl in Algiers* but to listen to it six nights running did nothing for my musical appreciation, and in fact it practically drove me mad. I asked friends each night and, as the week progressed, I retreated further and further to the rear of the box.

In 1990 Norman Lamont asked me whether I would be interested in taking over the chairmanship of the War Memorials Trust whose founder, Sir Donald Thompson, a Tory MP and long-serving Whip, was retiring. Donald was an attractive character and by profession a butcher. Above his shop in Yorkshire a sign bore the legend – MEAT TO PLEASE YER – PLEASED TO MEET YER! Donald had many sterling qualities but administration was not one of them and the charity was in a shaky condition. Its purpose was, and is, to facilitate the restoration of our nation's sixty thousand war memorials. Many of these lay abandoned by reason of redevelopment, being located in a wide range of contexts – bus shelters, hospitals, offices, fire stations – these buildings are constantly being swept away, requiring a new home for the memorials. More often the memorials simply need basic restoration.

I was attracted by this challenge and set about refinancing the charity and refashioning the Trustees. The refinancing was successfully achieved and, as is so often the case, the Sainsbury family were the largest contributors. As new Trustees I persuaded Gavin Stamp, Colin Amery and Richard Broyd to join, bringing their architectural and heritage gravitas to bear. The charity was scrupulously directed by Frances Moreton but I was persuaded to allow it to veer off along well-intentioned educational avenues that were not consonant with the original aim of the charity as laid down by Donald Thompson. I was also, ever the entrepreneur, exasperated by the politically-correct corporate governance agenda which seemed to occupy two-thirds of the Trustees' time. I therefore resigned amicably after twelve years, yielding the chairmanship to a robust and clever solicitor, Peter McCormick.

❧

I spent a considerable amount of time, whilst a Governor of Stowe School, serving as the Chairman of the appeal to save Stowe House and as a Trustee of the Stowe House Preservation Trust. I am not a committee man, subscribing to the theory that the best committee is comprised of two people, one of them absent. However, we scored some notable successes and, building on the foundations ably laid by Adrian Evans, a contemporary of mine and banking director of Lazards who died too young jogging, we achieved our objective and Stowe House was indeed restored. One of Britain's finest perspectives must be the view south from Stowe House across the lake to the Vanburgh Pavilions. Philistines had placed a nine-hole golf course slap in the middle of it, which has now been removed due to the generosity of a private benefactor.

Initially Sir Nigel Mobbs, the Chairman of Slough Estates, had served as Chairman of the Stowe House Preservation Trust. An indisputably able man, his fuse was in inverse proportion to his height (about 1.95 metres). One evening we gave a dinner for Prince Charles at Stowe and invited potential donors. From one of these guests, an Arab lady, we had high hopes of a substantial gift. Mobbs, Richard Kleinwort (another Governor) and I were greeting the guests and Mobbs was highly agitated at the prospect of welcoming Prince Charles. A limousine bearing our Arabian Princess arrived simultaneously with HRH, prompting Mobbs to bellow 'Move along, move along for goodness' sake!' at the bewildered Arabs.

'There goes £5 million,' Richard correctly observed.

It was said of Nigel Mobbs that when hospitalised he received a letter from the Company Secretary of Slough Estates, which read:

Dear Sir Nigel,
I have been commanded by your colleagues on the board to wish you a speedy recovery and return to work. This resolution was passed by six votes to four with three abstentions.

I spent too many years as a member of Stowe's Governing body, which was a fairly agreeable group. Though it was courteously and efficiently chaired by Nicholas Lyell, a Member of Parliament, I never felt comfortable as a member, partially because we never left a hermetically sealed room to visit the kitchens or the lavatories, not to mention the classrooms. There was an air of impending crisis too, which was eventually headed off, to their credit, by Christopher Honeyman Brown, Lyell's successor, and Anthony Wallersteiner, the present Headmaster. Two of our sons were there, neither of whom were happy or fulfilling their promise. We removed them, which afforded me the opportunity of removing myself. I was given a handsome John Piper sketch of the Gothic Temple as a thank-you, which I value.

๛

I have spent many happy days shooting and cannot understand why I am not better at it. I must have attended hundreds of shoots of varying quality and can scarcely recall an uncongenial day. I have enjoyed forty years of shooting at Blenheim, and many years at the legendary Gunnerside in North Yorkshire as a guest of Robert Miller. Bob, undeniably one of the most successful men of his generation – having founded the first duty free shop at Kai Tak Airport in Hong Kong in the 1950s – is an impressive individual, firm but fair. As well as being a first-class shot and host, with his South American wife Chantal, he is an outstanding yachtsman with many racing trophies to his credit. Thanks to the generosity of David Tang, I have shot at Alnwick, Garrowby and Arundel and recently at The Lakes with Richard Caring. Otherwise I have been fortunate to have shot regularly at Penshurst in Kent, King's Walden Bury in Hertfordshire and Stutton Hall in Suffolk with my good friends Philip de L'Isle, Tommy Pilkington and Henry Strutt.

I also shot for many years locally, near Sandwich in Kent. This was brilliantly orchestrated by Carel Mosselmans, accomplished sportsman and businessman, who not only created a challenging partridge shoot virtually from scratch but also managed to assemble outstandingly agreeable guns, many of them his Dutch relations. The only drawback was his attachment to an ex-public house, the venue for lunch. The gloomy lady presiding seemed more anxious to identify a reason to take offence than to provide friendly service. The shoot itself was conducted on the land owned by a handsome and cerebral peer who for some reason kept a couple of llamas in his garden. He occasionally made his aristocratic self known by standing behind the guns accompanied by a weird-looking dog, and would once in a while acknowledge our presence with a gracious word or two. He was very friendly with the Queen of Denmark and scored a rare miss when he asked all eight of the guns one by one whether they would like to dine with her that night. No thanks, we all said.

❧

It was whilst shooting with Richard Caring that Henry Wyndham, then Chairman of Sotheby's, told me that he had had an unusual experience shortly before. He had offered a job to a young man, George Percy, who had – to Henry's amazement – turned it down, preferring he said to work in the natural resources business. No one, Henry said, had ever before turned down the offer of a job at Sotheby's. He said complimentary things about George and it so happened that I had got myself interested in the geothermal potential of the UK and resolved to form a company – Cluff Geothermal – to pursue the concept. I met George and was impressed with his personality and energy. It was my intention to investigate the geothermal potential in the granite rocks in north-east England, where it so happened his family were landowners – so that was helpful too. George became the managing director and my wife joined the board alongside Sir Christopher Edwards and an academic. The usual British bureaucratic blocks were placed in front of our plans and George had the imagination to divert to Ethiopia where there obtained much better geothermal potential and far fewer busybodies.

❧

As an entrepreneur of some experience, which has now spanned fifty years in the UK, China and Africa, I diffidently set out some reflections and observations. In a general sense the value and status of the entrepreneur has advanced during those years. Indeed, in the 1950s and 60s I sensed that universities regarded business as an unsuitable destination for the brighter students, but that has certainly changed for the better.

Of the 1950s and 60s I would make two general points. Firstly to note the tremendous contribution to commerce that derived from the UK's policy of giving shelter to Jewish immigrants. So many of the country's successful enterprises in those years were the creation of such individuals – Thorn, Racal, GEC, a long and distinguished list. Secondly, immigrants apart (since many studied at German and Austrian universities), the successful home-grown businessmen were none of them university-trained, regardless of their social position. As examples I cite Jimmy Goldsmith, an old Etonian, and Nigel Broackes (Trafalgar House), an old Stowe boy, as is Richard Branson. The list is long.

I have earlier pointed out the past reluctance of executives to leave the major oil companies to form their own venture with City support, which would indeed have been on offer. That trend has changed and entrepreneurs in the UK are highly charged, although there now obtains a tendency for the brightest students to join the investment banking and hedge fund industries. Cerebral and important as they undoubtedly are, their high salaries possibly deflect many would-be entrepreneurs from establishing businesses that employ people and actually make things.

I am often asked what attributes an entrepreneur needs to be successful, particularly in the natural resources sector. Frankly the elements that are necessary, if not essential, to render an individual entrepreneurial are self-evident, but first of all comes the capacity to be decisive. That capacity and the ability to act quickly is very rare in people. Decisions need to be complemented by energy and imagination. I would add that resilience in the face of frequent disappointment is a further strength. As far as navigating one's way through the various complexities of negotiation is concerned, there is no doubt that good manners always prevail. I am constantly amazed by how patronising some Europeans and Americans still are in an African context.

∾

Looking back over the past fifty years I find it very puzzling to account for the failure of so many British institutions. After all, our private education system remains a byword the world over. So why did Lloyd's of London, for example, disintegrate? The concatenation of dishonesty and incompetence which emerged from the wreckage is baffling. I do believe that overly high taxation was part of the reason, but certainly not an excuse.

I escaped membership of Lloyd's by a strange chance. Sitting in the Officers' Mess of the 1st Battalion of the Grenadier Guards one evening, my brother officer Patrick Lichfield came in looking uncharacteristically down. I asked him what the matter was and he revealed that his father had just lost a large amount of money by reason of his membership of Lloyd's and 5,000 acres of Staffordshire had to be sold (to his great credit he subsequently bought them all back). That was 1963. Many years later, when constantly pressed by various Lloyd's agents to sign up, usually with the assurance that 'nothing can go wrong old boy', I recalled my friend's experience and declined. My mother, however, did succumb (largely because, by an anomaly, income from membership was judged to be 'earned' and therefore taxed at a much lower rate than unearned income, as it was then termed). Once a year she was patronised at a lunch at the Savoy with other names and that was the only contact she had with her agent until everything went wrong and he emerged as the only member with a stop loss policy. Not a word of apology or explanation.

I wonder whether the recommendations

of the Cadbury and Greenbury commit-
tees would have made any difference to the
Lloyd's debacle? This explosion of corporate
governance regulations seems to me to have
served very little useful purpose, other than
the boon it has been to the headhunting
industry. It would be interesting to analyse the
performance of the large business combines
that have conformed to corporate governance requirements by not only separating the
role of Chairman and Chief Executive but,
incredibly, in many cases appointing both of
these from outside. In my humble view the
Chairman and Chief Executive should not
only understand the business but also all of
the senior people in it. What kind of signal
does it send to your staff when you make it
plain that an existing employee can never
aspire to one of the top jobs in the business?
And equally, what should investors make of
a company which has no faith in its own
management, but rather feels it necessary
to conduct an external search every time a
vacancy occurs?

Another governance objective was to end
the habit of cosy boards where friendship
obtains, possibly to the disadvantage of the
shareholders. But is it not the case that it is
inevitable that if you work together, sharing
the ups or downs of commercial experience,
you will become friends? And do you not let
your friends down last of all? Whereas the

adversarial form of governance is much more likely to lead to the executives becoming secretive, which is when the trouble starts. The finest discipline I have had as an Executive Chairman of long standing is that I would die rather than embarrass my colleagues – precisely because they *are* friends.

The Government have also seen fit to pass the Bribery Act. To me it is an insulting piece of legislation in that it is implicit that we executives have a tendency to be corrupt. This has spawned more red tape and as far as I am aware has not led to the prosecution of a single businessman. What has happened is the usual law of unintended consequences, as non-executives become like dead hands, anxious as they are of the risk of prosecution. At the very least non-executives should be released from the threat of legal action.

૭

In 1969 I bought a house on top of the White Cliffs of Dover. I have scarcely spent an unhappy hour there since. With a 180-degree view of the English Channel, the veranda is without a doubt my favourite place. It was built in 1926, rather improbably by Sir William Beardswell, who had been High Sheriff of Madras, and designed by Geoffrey Lucas, a pupil of Voysey. Sir William was something of an ecologist and required Lucas to add a functioning windmill to the house to provide it with electricity. The base of that windmill is my octagonal library, which houses my collection of principally African and military books. From there on a clear day one can see the clock in Calais, and the house is deemed to be the closest in England to Europe. My wife and I, after our marriage and the addition of three children, have significantly extended the house by adding a large drawing-room, a second dining room and two more bedrooms. This has been achieved without any damage to the integrity of the original design. Although we did the work ourselves, with the assistance of an excellent local builder, C. J. Gray, we did retain the architect, historian and Lutyens expert Roderick Gradidge at the suggestion of Gavin Stamp, a friend from the *Spectator*. Roderick was an extraordinary figure who wore his hair in a waist-length ponytail, and although stocky and thoroughly 'butch' in appearance, he insisted on wearing a skirt. The combination of the skirt and the upper-class military modulation ('The country's going to the dogs – hrrumph!') created an arresting and unforgettable effect. Notwithstanding his bizarre appearance, he was most intelligent and entertaining company. He died very young.

The Windmill's visitors' book attests to a certain diversity of friendship, although it is dominated by Paddy Pakenham and Nicholas

Berry and, until their deaths, Mickie and Laura Brand. One welcome guest was a beautiful and brilliant German girl, Andrea von Stumm, with whom I did live, in Eaton Square, for a year. I also travelled with her to Hong Kong, Singapore and New York and I could not have wished for a more loyal and stimulating companion. However, the young ladies ceased appearing after my marriage in 1993! Mickie Brand I miss very much. An Etonian and Coldstream Guards officer in the War, he became a most admired rare book dealer at Marlborough Rare Books. He was devoted to his wife, Laura, who drowned whilst swimming in the sea off the Bahamas. Poor Mickie went into a long decline and died three years ago.

Many of my close friends lived in Sandwich Bay in those days and most weekends in the summer we visited each other's houses. In many respects objects are preferable to people because they never change, they are constant. That house has been a constant friend and home to me and my family, together with my books, for fifty years.

Books have been my favourite companions – war, travel, crime and Wodehouse being most prominent in my library. At one time when I spent many months travelling in Africa my briefcase always contained a box of Havana cigars, a revolver and a novel by P. G. Wodehouse.

West Indian lawyer aged thirty-three. She was then the head of the legal department at Lazard Brothers & Co, the merchant bank in London. Possessed of great beauty, formidable intelligence and a strong disposition, she has now been my wife for almost twenty-five years and we have three sons whose existence amply justifies our presence on earth. They have contrasting personalities and we are very proud of them. The video of our wedding will attest to the fact that my, by then, wife had completely forgotten my name is John and that 'Algy' is in fact a nickname I have borne since my school days, thanks to the movie *The Importance of Being Earnest*. In 2012 I had to undergo a hernia operation and as I was about to be rendered unconscious a male nurse said to me, 'Your name, John ducky?!' Those could have been the last words I heard!

At the age of seventy-five I look back with some astonishment that I touched life at so many different points, as I continue to do. I write these closing words at the same desk, in the same study, overlooking the same sea, in the same house in which I have worked and read for fifty years, and from which I have sallied forth on many adventures.

Index